POWER HOUSE

A LEGACY

STEPH ADAMS

There will come a time in everyone's journey, where you have to leave behind the person you once were and step into your own power to become who you were truly meant to be.

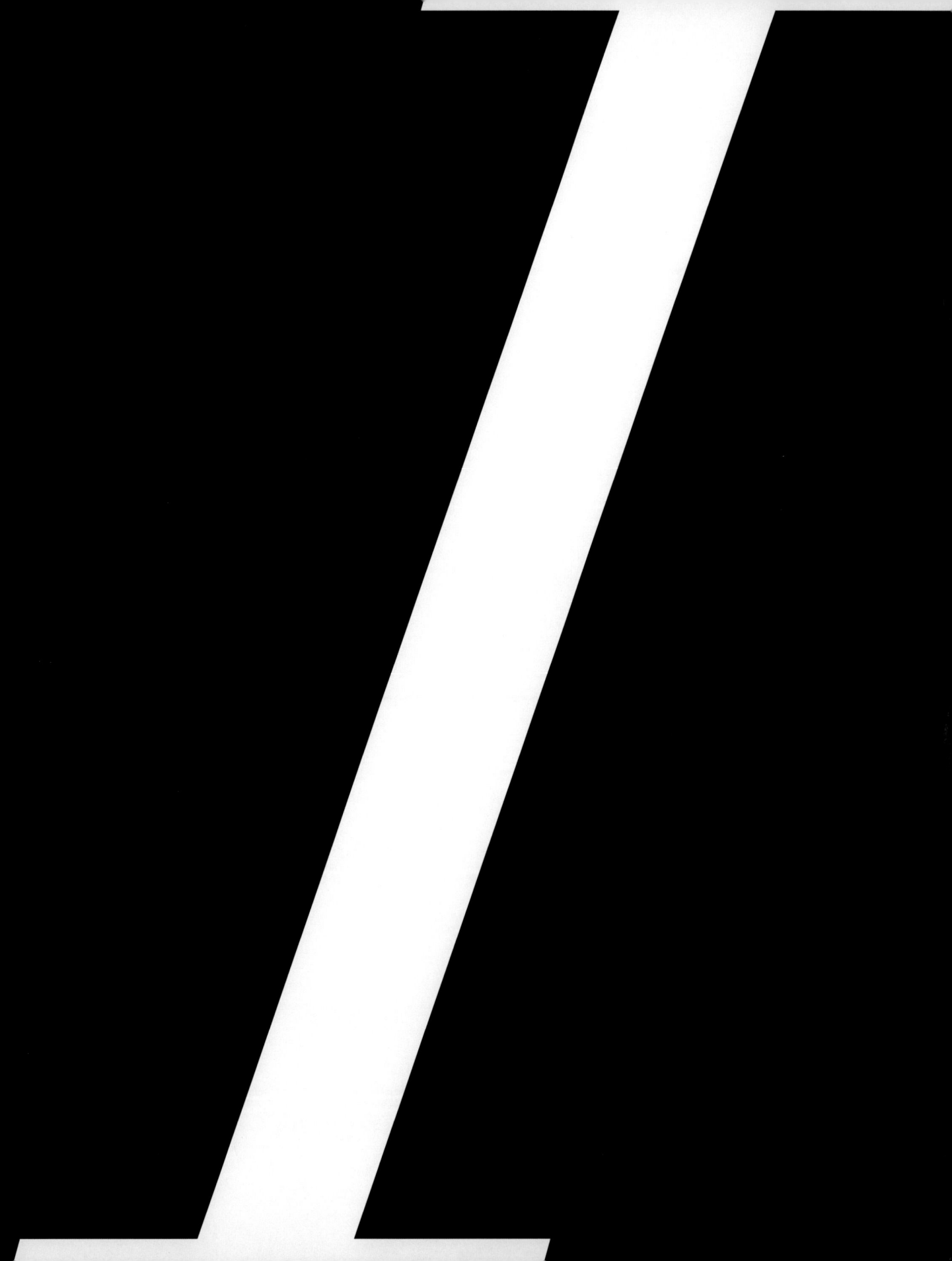

It is not the critic who counts; not the man who points out how the strong man stumbles, or where the doer of deeds could have done them better. The credit belongs to the man who is actually in the arena, whose face is marred by dust and sweat and blood; who strives valiantly; who errs, who comes short again and again, because there is no effort without error and shortcoming; but who does actually strive to do the deeds; who knows great enthusiasms, the great devotions; who spends himself in a worthy cause; who at the best knows in the end the triumph of high achievement, and who at the worst, if he fails, at least fails while daring greatly; so that his place shall never be with those cold and timid souls who neither know victory nor defeat.

THEODORE ROOSEVELT

POWER HOUSE

A LEGACY

STEPH ADAMS

LONDON ❋ CAMBRIDGE ❋ NEW YORK ❋ SHARJAH

*To my mother, sister Jules and all my family for
your love and support over the years.*

*To all the men and women who are
brave enough to follow
your dreams...*

Your time is now.

Photography: Hana le Van

AUTHOR

Award-winning author, model, art director and businesswoman Steph Adams is a highly distinguished name in the fashion and publishing industry. She has become an inspiration to women worldwide, authoring nineteen published books, eighteen of them bestsellers, and winning two prestigious awards for her work in women's empowerment, featuring diverse voices globally and her commitment to inclusivity and representation. She has also contributed to various charities.

Appearing on billboards in New York Times Square and West Hollywood, Los Angeles, Adams has graced magazine covers from *Harper's Bazaar*, *Grazia*, *Forbes*, *Time* and international editions of *L'Officiel*.

After first launching into the digital space in 2010, Steph has gone on to build a global network, contributing as an Ambassador for various luxury brands and attending red-carpet events from Dior, Louis Vuitton and the Venice and Cannes film festivals.

Born and raised in Perth, Western Australia, Steph Adams began modelling at the age of twelve, modelling internationally around the world for a decade before finishing her Bachelor of Arts Degree and working as an Art Director for retail giant *Net-a-Porter* and magazine publications such as *British Vogue*, *Harper's Bazaar*, *Elle*, *Marie Claire*, *Vogue Australia* and *Condé Nast Traveller*.

Adams has made a significant impact by contributing to various fields, such as luxury, fashion, style, philanthropy, beauty, success and wellness. Adams continues to work across international projects.

"In a world where empowerment and creativity intersect, Steph Adams stands as a guiding light, inspiring others to embrace their unique voices and stories. Her legacy as a visionary, uplifting women through diverse storytelling, will undoubtedly leave an indelible mark on the fashion industry and beyond."

FORBES, UK, 2024

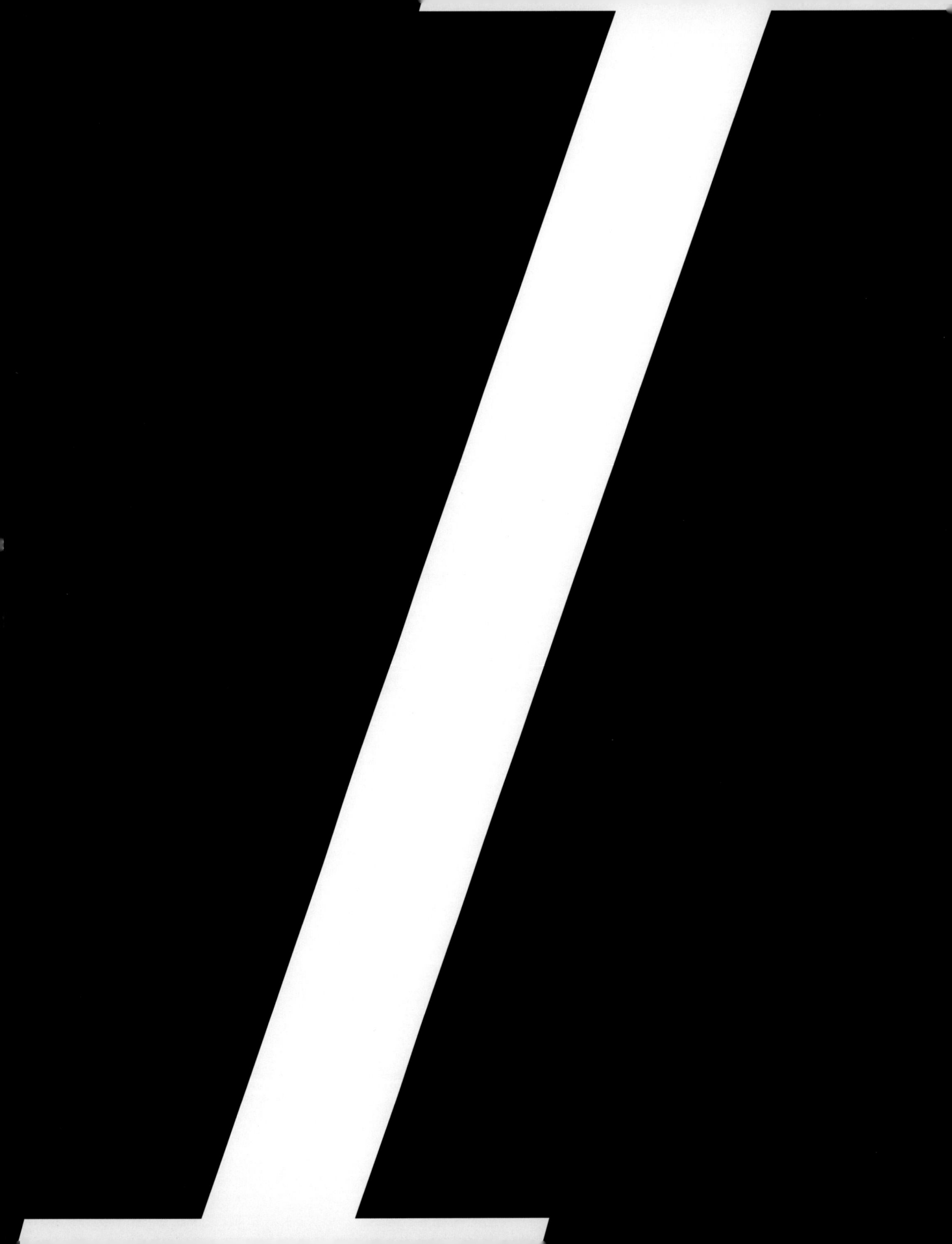

*IF YOU WANT
TO BE SUCCESSFUL
IN BUSINESS,
YOU HAVE TO
BE WILLING TO BE
MISUNDERSTOOD FOR
LONG PERIODS
OF TIME.*

JEFF BEZOS

Photography: Matteo Colson

INTRODUCTION

Being a Powerhouse in today's world takes courage, determination, a strong sense of self, passion, hard work, perseverance and sacrifice. *Powerhouse* is the book that showcases and recognises all iconic men and women who are successful in their fields. These men and women give their valuable advice from what they have experienced along their journeys, helping you to take action and to know that even during setbacks you can continue to persevere forward with the same determination.

Success is vital for providing confidence, leadership, a sense of wellbeing, hope and the ability to give back to a community. It is what creates drive and purpose in today's society. Success is what is required to continue to live a life of passion.

When we are driven by a deep sense of purpose and an unwavering desire to make a difference, our passion can become a powerful force for change. By channelling our passion, we can inspire others, challenge and bring about transformative outcomes.

Whether they are working to build big businesses, working for charities, creating a more equitable society, or they are demonstrating what leaders can do with a strong belief and commitment to creating a long-lasting legacy.

Powerhouse shares valuable advice for succeeding in business and in life. Around the world more and more people from a young age are establishing the resilient attributes of what makes a Powerhouse today. Featuring over sixty interviews, you will hear from:

Clint Eastwood, Cayetano Riviera, Scott Steindorf, Princess Jahnavi Kumari Mewar of India, Susie Wolff, HRH Prince Nereides Antonio Giamundo de Bourbon, Sharlette Hambrick, Novlene Mills, Rosanna Scotto, Elle Macpherson, Delphine Jelk, Tatiana Blatnik, Lauren Bush and more.

The key to success is to keep going, keep pushing, keep striving and keep believing, no matter what. By carving out a long lasting career in your field and following your passion, you can create a life-long legacy, something you will leave for your children and your grandchildren in years to come.

This is a timeless book that will inspire generations to come.

STEPH ADAMS

FOREWORD

I first met Steph Adams at the Hotel de Crillon in Paris in September 2021. I was struck by a sense of familiarity that transcended mere introductions. From the moment we sat down to talk, I felt as though I had known her for years. It was as if we were kindred spirits, united in our fervent advocacy for women's empowerment. Steph exudes a rare blend of grace and strength, embodying the very essence of resilience and determination. Her passion and dedication to women's empowerment shone through in every word she spoke.

As we delved into discussions on empowering women to embrace their true potential, I couldn't help but be inspired by her unwavering commitment to this cause and her presence. Her passion was palpable, igniting a fire within me to strive for greater heights in championing gender equality. It was inspiring to hear about her journey and the challenges she has overcome along the way.

Steph is a true advocate for change, using her platform to uplift and inspire women from all walks of life. She has truly created a platform like no other, where women from diverse backgrounds come together to share their stories and experiences. In her latest book, she continues this mission of showcasing the voices of women from different cultures and countries around the world.

Through insightful interviews and shared conversations, Steph Adams highlights the strength and resilience of these remarkable women. She brings attention to their achievements in various fields, inspiring others with their journeys.

As we delve into this new chapter of empowering global conversations, it's clear that Steph Adams is not only a writer but also a champion for female empowerment. Her work serves as a reminder that when women support each other across borders and boundaries, incredible things can happen.

Meeting Steph Adams was not just a chance encounter; it was a transformative experience that left an indelible mark on my journey towards advocating for women's rights. Her wisdom and insight have enriched my perspective, reinforcing my belief in the power of unity and solidarity among women. Steph's powerful aura left a lasting impression on me, motivating me to continue my own work towards gender equality. It reaffirmed my conviction that together, we can break barriers and pave the way for a more inclusive society where every woman is empowered to thrive. Steph's influence will continue to resonate within me, fuelling my passion for driving positive change in the world and reinforcing my belief that together, we can create real change - one step at a time.

Sincerely yours,

HRH Prince Nereides Antonio Giamundo de Bourbon
Chairman
NEREIDES DE BOURBON GROUP
Paris, France

> *EVERY WOMAN'S SUCCESS SHOULD BE AN INSPIRATION TO ANOTHER, WE'RE STRONGEST WHEN WE CHEER EACH OTHER ON.*

SERENA WILLIAMS

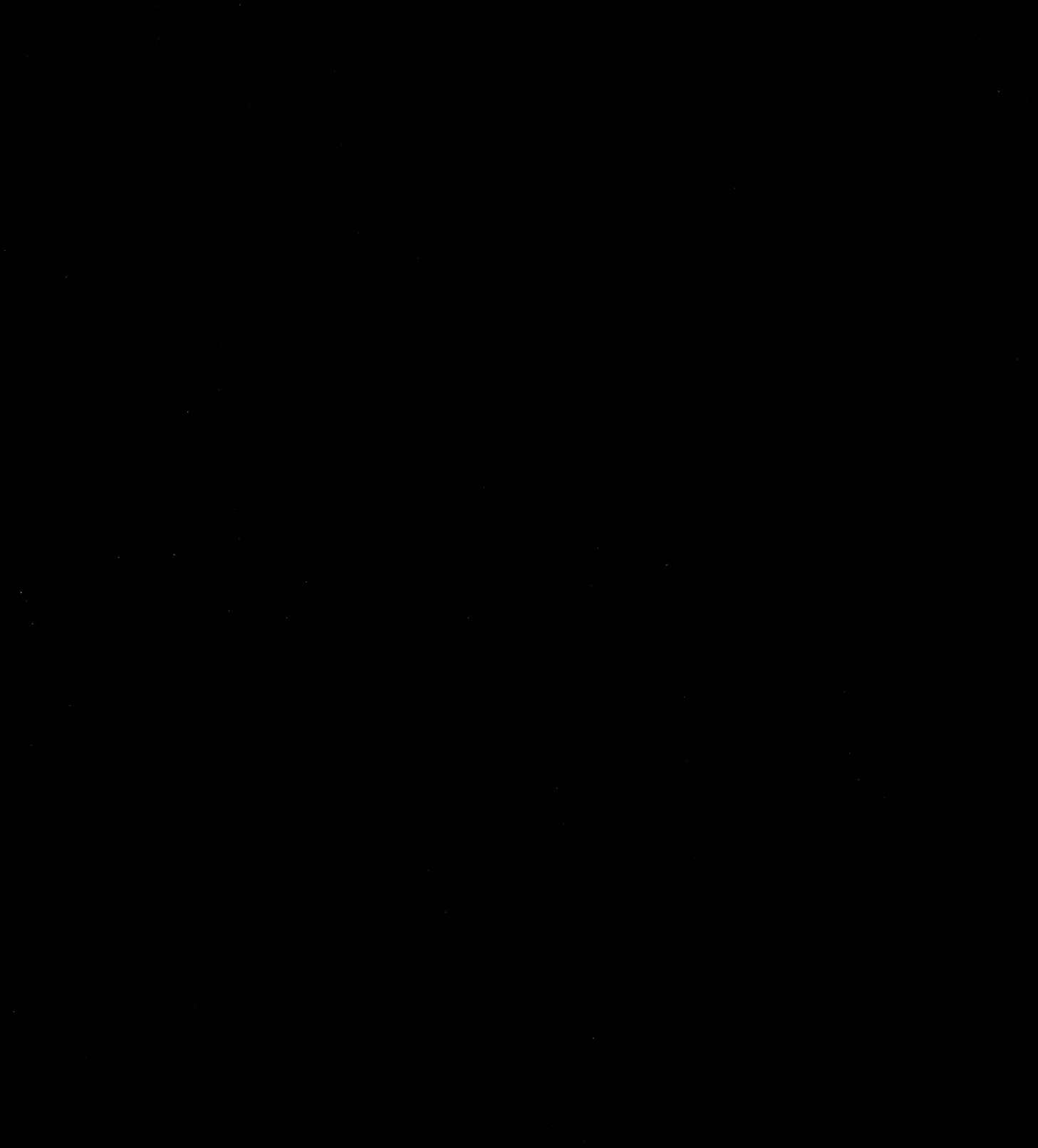

This book is dedicated to all the Powerhouse men and women around the world that continue to keep going even in the face of challenges and diversity. Keep going, keep on striving in the direction of your dreams and goals.

For Bailey and Joshua

CONTENTS

34   Clint Eastwood
American Actor, Filmmaker, Musician, and Politician

43   HRH Prince Nereides Antonio Giamundo De Bourbon
Cultural Diplomat, Grand Couturier, Publisher Of L'Époque

49   Cayetano Rivera
Spanish Torero Bullfighter

53   Georges Tomb
Award-Winning Composer and Concert Pianist

57   Scott Steindorff
American Film Producer

60   Novlene Mills
World Championship Medallist I Track & Field Athlete

65   Princess Jahnavi Kumari Mewar
Founder and Head of Private Equity Auctus Fora

68   Susie Wolff
Former Professional Racing Driver and Current Managing Director of F1 Academy

74   Sharlette Hambrick
Emmy award-winning News and Entertainment Producer

78   Rosanna Scotto
Host of "Good Day New York" on FOX 5

83   Delphine Jelk
Perfumer for Guerlain

87   Tatiana Blatnik
Entrepreneur, Founder of Breathe

92   Nadine Mirada
Supermodel and Guess Model

96   Lauren Bush
CEO and Co-Founder of FEED Projects

99   Charlotte Tilbury
Makeup Artist and Founder of Charlotte Tilbury

106   Elle Macpherson
Businesswoman, Supermodel, Mother, Co-Founder of WelleCo

111   Karen Gee
Entrepreneur and Fashion Designer

117   Olivia Palermo
Entrepreneur

123   Abeer Stouhi
Founder of Glamoda

129   Leanne Robers
Co-Founder of She Loves Tech

133   Bria Fleming
Fashion Designer, Reality TV Star, Fashion Icon

135   Leonie Hanne
Fashion Influencer

141   Paris Hilinski
Fashion Icon, Golfing Pro

145   Marianna Hewitt
Co-Founder, Summer Fridays

148   Hofit Golan
Fashion Influencer

153   Celia Walden
British Journalist, Editor-At-Large, Author

157   Rachel Zoe
Fashion Designer, Stylist, Businesswoman

163   Tash Oakley
Founder of A Bikini A Day, Monday Swimwear & Monday Active

171   India Hicks
Founder & Creative Director at India Hicks Inc.

174   Aerin Lauder
Founder and Creative Director of Aerin

179   Laura Gallon
Jewellery Designer

185   Jo Malone
Founder of Jo Loves

189   Paula Brezavscek
Founder of Azala Skin Clinic, Miami

195   Kathryn Eisman
Television Host, *Undressed with Kathryn Eisman* Author, Founder, High Heel Jungle

199 Negin Mirsalehi
Influencer, Beauty Entrepreneur,
Creator of Hair Care Brand Gisou

205 Irene Krauze
Founder of Bequartii

208 Samantha Brett
Bestselling Author, Founder of Naked Sundays

213 Alexandra McGuigan
Founder & CEO, Inclusive Asset Management

217 Viivi Avellan
Co-Founder of Viilee Solutions LLC

221 Gay Gassmann
Contributing Editor of Architectural Digest USA,
Vogue Arabia, Vogue Arabia Living and Ad China

226 Noella Coursaris Musunka
Founder of Malaika

233 Laurie Adams
President of Women for Women International

239 Melissa Odabash
Fashion Designer

245 Kristin Cavallari
Founder and CEO of Uncommon James,
New York Times Bestselling Author

249 Monique Lhuillier
Fashion Designer

257 Jennifer Fisher
Jewellery Entrepreneur

261 Leesa Evans
Hollywood Costume Designer and Stylist

265 Eleonora Lastrucci
Fashion Designer

271 Candice Lake
Style Editor, Model, Photographer, Blogger

275 Angela Ventsel
Founder and CEO of estx

281 Helene Benhamou
Singer

282 Koukla Lapidus
French Actor

287 Natalie De'Banco
Creative Director of Bronx and Banco

291 Kristina Bazan
Social Influencer, Creator of Kayture.com

297 Megan Hess
International Fashion Illustrator

301 Ella Mills
Bestselling Author and Health Entrepreneur

305 Amanda Harrigan
Founder of Global Matchmaking Service Hytch

309 Pia Cooke
Head of Advisory Solutions,
Global Wealth Management

313 Christina Mantoura Gough
Business Woman and Founder of the
Hot Tub & Swim Spa Company

319 Emma Jane Pilkington
Interior Designer

323 Samantha Wills
Jewellery Entrepreneur and Founder
of the Samantha Wills Foundation

329 Jess Sepel
Bestselling Author and Nutritionist

335 Elizabeth Dart
Entrepreneur, Founder of Hunter & Queen

339 Bobbi Brown
Makeup Artist and Founder of
Bobbi Brown Cosmetics

343 Tamara Ralph
Creative Director and Co-Founder
of Ralph & Russo

348 Dr Barbara Sturm
Skincare Entrepreneur

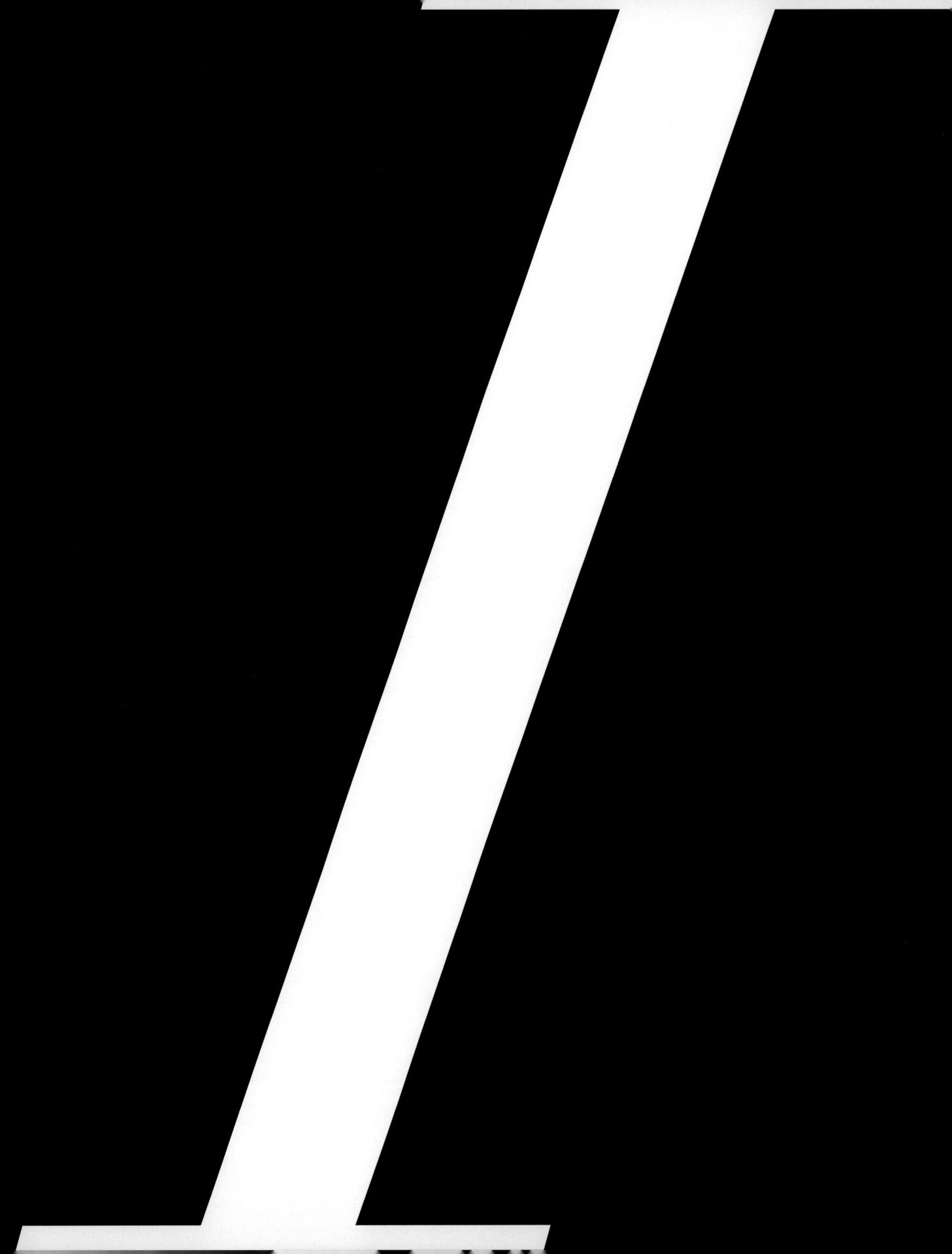

*IT'S KIND OF
FUN TO DO
THE IMPOSSIBLE.*

WALT DISNEY

CLINT EASTWOOD

AMERICAN ACTOR, FILMMAKER, MUSICIAN, AND POLITICIAN

Four-time Academy Award recipient Clint Eastwood is one of the most renowned film directors in the world.

STEPH: What were your interests as a young boy?
CLINT: You know what, it was a different time then. It was the depression and we moved around a lot. Our main goal was to stay alive.

STEPH: Tell us your story how you started your career into acting/films.
CLINT: I was in junior high and my English teacher appointed me as the lead in the school play. I think she gave it to me more of a punishment than an award, to keep me out of trouble. I remember being so nervous because we had to perform for the High Schoolers. Honestly, I was scared shitless. I was a little kid and they seemed so much older. I ended up doing okay; actually, I got a lot of laughs. It ended up being a hit, but I will never do that again.

STEPH: One of your biggest career highlights?
CLINT: You know what… All of it! I have worked hard but I have also been very lucky. It has been one hell of a ride!

STEPH: What has been your biggest success?
CLINT: Unforgiven was a huge turning point in my career.

STEPH: What is your definition of a powerhouse?
CLINT: A hard worker.

STEPH: What makes you take on a story to produce into a film?
CLINT: I like to make stories that leave you thinking. Whether it is good or bad, happy or sad, something that resonates, and you can't shake it. Something that stays with you.

STEPH: What do you think you would be doing if you were not directing films?
CLINT: Maybe something with the Parks Department.

STEPH: How do you think acting and directing changed your perspective on life and films?
CLINT: I've learned that you really can't control anything. So, I just try to enjoy myself whatever it is I am doing.

STEPH: What are your top success tips to others wanting advice?
CLINT: Never give up. Stick with it.

STEPH: What is your motto?
CLINT: Believe in yourself, even if you're the only one.

HRH PRINCE NEREIDES ANTONIO GIAMUNDO DE BOURBON

CULTURAL DIPLOMAT, GRAND COUTURIER, PUBLISHER OF L'ÉPOQUE

HRH Prince Nereides Antonio Giamundo de Bourbon is a cultural diplomat, financial strategist, founder of Parisian haute couture house Nereides de Bourbon and publisher of media giant L'Époque *magazine.*

Growing up in a family that revered literature, aesthetics, and art, my childhood was a vibrant tapestry woven with creativity and intellectual curiosity. From a young age, I found myself enchanted by the world of literature, diving into poems that spoke to my soul while also expressing my own thoughts through writing. I was equally captivated by visual arts; my room was a sanctuary filled with drawing sheets where I honed my skills in sketching human silhouettes before transitioning to fashion illustration.

Music played a pivotal role as well; starting piano lessons early on, I discovered the joy of expressing emotions through melodies. This blend of rationality and passion defined my personality, allowing me to explore diverse interests without ever feeling confined to one path. As I matured, my love for the humanities led me to pursue studies in literature and philosophy, while simultaneously studying law and nurturing my creative side through fashion design techniques. This duality has not only shaped my identity but has also fuelled an insatiable thirst for knowledge, which continues to inspire my journey today. This relentless pursuit of knowledge and creativity laid the groundwork for my aspirations, leading me to seek experiences that would further broaden my horizons. I embraced opportunities to engage in community projects that combined art with social advocacy, believing fervently in the power of creative expression as a vehicle for change.

CAREER DIVERSITY

Navigating a career that spans cultural diplomacy, fashion design, ballet, jewellery branding, and skincare can seem daunting, but each step has been a vital chapter in my journey. As a cultural diplomat, I learned the art of communication and the importance of building bridges between diverse communities. This experience ignited my passion for creativity, leading me to explore fashion design, where I expressed my visions through art.

Transitioning into jewellery and skincare branding allowed me to merge aesthetics with personal care, crafting products that resonate emotionally with consumers. My time as a ballet dancer is still instilling discipline and grace, reinforcing my belief in the power of storytelling through movement. Finally, stepping into the world of global publishing through L'Époque magazine felt like a natural progression; it provided a platform to share diverse narratives and celebrate creativity on a larger scale. Each role not only contributed to my skill set but also shaped my world view, allowing me to connect with people from all walks of life. Embracing this diversity has enriched my work and fuelled my passion for storytelling in all its forms.

PASSION FOR CREATIVITY

Growing up surrounded by beauty, my admiration for fashion designers set the foundation for my journey into haute couture. Each stroke of my pencil on countless sketches reflected a dream that began in my childhood. Even while studying law at university, I found solace in designing women's clothing, filling my notes with ideas and inspirations that danced between the lines of legal theory and artistic expression. My fascination with the fluidity of fabrics and their ability to embody intellect inspired me to create garments that tell a story.

In 2007, I took a bold step by founding my Parisian couture house, Nereides de Bourbon. This endeavour became a testament to my passion and creativity, establishing a brand that resonates with elegance and sophistication. The culmination of my efforts has led to my designs gracing the red carpets of major events in Los Angeles, Cannes, Rome, and Venice, where they have been embraced by celebrities who appreciate the artistry behind haute couture. Each piece is not just clothing; it's an embodiment of dreams, heritage, and a celebration of femininity—a jewel I cherish alongside my beloved magazine L'Époque, which I proudly carry forward with respect for its rich history.

As I navigate this vibrant world of haute couture, I realise that every garment I create transcends mere fabric and thread; it becomes a vessel for emotion and expression.

The process of bringing an idea to life is akin to crafting a narrative, where each design is a chapter filled with intricate details that reflect not only individual stories but also collective experiences. Collaborating with skilled artisans who share my vision has been instrumental in refining my craft—each stitch woven with dedication and an unyielding commitment to perfection. It is in these moments that I understand the profound impact fashion can have, acting as a bridge between cultures and eras, showcasing the timeless elegance that resonates deeply within the human spirit. This journey isn't merely about aesthetics; it's about creating connections, inspiring confidence, and honouring the diverse narratives that define beauty in all its forms.

CAREER TURNING POINT

There have been a few essential moments in my life that have shaped who I am today. The first significant turning point was when I made the decision to start living on my own at the age of nineteen. It was a crucial step for me to break away from my family and learn to rely solely on my own strength and independence. Living between Paris, Capri, and Florence allowed me to explore the world and understand the true value of things and sacrifice.

In 2007, I achieved a lifelong dream by inaugurating my Haute Couture house. This moment filled me with pride and joy as I realised that I had succeeded on my own merits. Ten years later, however, 2017 presented me with challenges that forced me to assert my individuality and face difficult choices, ultimately leading to a profound change in my personality and priorities. At that time my family ties were also put under hard stress but time and my own compassion have since healed many wounds.

The end of 2019 brought sweetness into my life as I began sharing it with the person I love, who has always inspired and supported me. But it was in 2024 that a physical injury changed my life and personality forever, making me mentally stronger and more appreciative of life.

Looking ahead, 2025 is set to be the most important year of my life as I prepare to marry the person who has been by my side for the past twenty years. My love story is undoubtedly the greatest accomplishment of my life of which I am most proud and jealous along with my freedom.

COUTURE HOUSE NEREIDES DE BOURBON AND L'ÉPOQUE MAGAZINE

As I approach my fortieth birthday, I've made a conscious decision to channel my energy into two passions: the haute couture house Nereides de Bourbon and the illustrious magazine L'Époque. After eighteen transformative years in haute couture, I find myself at a creative crossroads, drawing inspiration from a multitude of sources as I craft two new collections—one destined for the chic streets of Paris and the other for the sun-kissed shores of Capri.

Simultaneously, I take immense pride in my role as the publishing director of L'Époque, a historic gem that I acquired in 2022. With roots dating back to 1845, L'Époque has been a bastion of freedom and progressive thought, often standing firm against manipulation and oppression, as evidenced by its bold public denunciation of historical figures like Hitler. This legacy is not just a testament to resilience but also an embodiment of our collective cultural heritage. As I nurture both my fashion endeavours and this illustrious publication, I am committed to honouring the past while embracing the future, ensuring that both Nereides de Bourbon and L'Époque continue to inspire and provoke thought in an ever-changing world.

QUALITIES FOR SUCCESS

To achieve true success, it's essential to cultivate a blend of qualities that not only elevate your personal achievements but also foster respect and love in your relationships. First and foremost, lucidity—clarity of thought and purpose— enables you to navigate challenges and make informed decisions. This clarity is often paired with resilience, the ability to bounce back from setbacks and learn from failures. Additionally, effective advocacy skills are crucial; being able to communicate your ideas passionately while respecting others' viewpoints fosters collaboration and builds strong networks.

Empathy plays a vital role as well; understanding and valuing others' perspectives engenders respect, which in turn creates an environment where love can flourish. A successful individual also embodies integrity, ensuring that their actions align with their values, thereby earning the trust of those around them. Lastly, a commitment to lifelong learning allows for personal growth and adaptation in an ever-changing world. By combining these qualities, you not only pave your path to success but also inspire those around you to strive for their own greatness.

CHALLENGES

On June 22, 2024, the night before my ballet performance at the Casino de Paris Theatre, disaster struck. A terrible injury left my right leg unusable, shattering my dreams in an instant. The initial diagnosis was grim – I would never walk or dance again. The sense of helplessness and fear was overwhelming.

But I refused to accept defeat. Through months of gruelling rehabilitation and unwavering determination, I defied the odds. Today, I walk again and have even returned to dancing. The road to recovery has been long and painful, but I am stronger for it.

As I prepare to perform once more, I am reminded that life is full of obstacles. But it is our resilience in the face of adversity that defines us. I have embraced the challenges and emerged a better, happier person.

I am proof that what doesn't break us only makes us stronger. I carry with me the belief that every setback is merely a setup for a comeback. I am ready to take the stage once more, not just for myself, but for everyone who has faced their own moments of defeat and found the strength to rise again. Life is a beautiful journey, and I am grateful for every step along the way.

LESSONS

As I reflect on my youth, a blend of tenderness and nostalgia washes over me. There were countless moments of joy intertwined with complex trials that shaped who I am today. If I could speak to that young boy, I would emphasise the importance of self-acceptance. You should take immense pride in who you are—your quirks, your passions, and your dreams. Embrace your uniqueness and not be afraid to let your true self shine through. It's important not to mould yourself to fit others' expectations, but rather to stay authentic and true to your own values and beliefs.

Don't waste time trying to please others at all costs; their approval is fleeting, but your authenticity is what truly matters. Life is too short to spend it trying to please others at the cost of our own happiness. We only get one shot at this journey called life, so it's crucial to prioritize our own well-being and fulfilment. Life is a singular journey, unique to you, and it is vital to embrace every facet of it. Remember, you have the right to pursue happiness without hesitation or fear. Additionally, recognise your inherent goodness and generosity; these traits will not only enrich your own life but also positively impact those around you. These qualities are not defined by external validation, but rather by the way you treat yourself and others with kindness and compassion. You are talented beyond measure, and as you navigate through life's challenges, hold onto the belief that you are worthy of love and success. Be gentle with yourself and know that every experience contributes to the remarkable person you will become. Your journey is yours alone, so cherish it fiercely. Finally, I am very proud of you.

PERSONAL CHALLENGES

Being myself. I think this is the hardest thing to achieve, a total inner balance and consistency between who we are and what we do. Navigating the journey of being yourself can often feel like an uphill battle. One of the most significant challenges I've faced is the constant pressure from external expectations—whether they come from society, family, or even friends. This pressure can create a dissonance between who you truly are and the persona you project to the world. For years, I struggled with this conflict, feeling like I had to mould myself to fit into predefined roles that didn't resonate with my authentic self. However, as I matured, I began to cultivate self-love and acceptance. I learned to listen closely to my own needs and desires, which meant acknowledging my flaws and forgiving myself for past mistakes. This journey has not been easy; it required immense inner work to achieve a sense of balance and consistency in my life. Yet, through this process, I have come to appreciate the power of being true to myself.

Embracing who I am—imperfections and all—has been one of the most liberating experiences of my life, allowing me to finally align my actions with my true self. I gradually learned to love, respect and forgive myself!

INSPIRATION

While I can't pinpoint a single person who has inspired me, I've always found motivation in those I perceive as being further along in their journeys—whether in knowledge, skills, creativity, or mindset. I consider myself a thief of inspiration;

I absorb the brilliance of others with my mind and eyes, striving to incorporate their strengths into my own growth.

This relentless pursuit of improvement fuels my evolution.

I've come to realise that true intelligence often lies in the willingness to adapt and change one's beliefs, while ignorance clings stubbornly to outdated notions. My curiosity drives me towards the unknown, transforming bewilderment into new insights. Adopting a dancer's critical eye, I observe others closely, analysing their missteps to avoid making the same mistakes myself. Failure is an inevitable part of growth, but by learning from the failures of those around me, I can navigate my path more wisely. In this way, every interaction becomes a lesson, every encounter a chance for growth. So, embrace your inspirations—past and present—and let them guide you on your journey toward continual self-improvement.

DEFINING MOMENT

Reflecting on my career, one defining moment stands out vividly: the invitation to speak at the historic Bachelard amphitheatre of Panthéon-Sorbonne University in December 2022. It was a remarkable occasion where I had the opportunity to share my journey with a new generation of bright students. Throughout my career, I have addressed large audiences, received accolades like the Nikolai Gogol Award from the Ukrainian government in 2022 for my diplomatic efforts during the early months of the war in Ukraine as well as the Who is Who International Award at the category 'World Eminent Man in Cultural Diplomacy & Finance", and even earned recognition from the National Chamber for Italian Fashion as the "Best Fashion Designer of the Year" in 2011 with the Santo Versace Award, just to name a few. Many other awards and honours have been bestowed on me in the financial, artistic and philanthropic fields. However, standing in front of those eager students made me realise that all my achievements had culminated in this moment of meaningful connection. It was not just about sharing my successes; it was about inspiring others to pursue their dreams passionately. Being acknowledged at such a prestigious institution validated my life's work and filled me with immense pride. It reinforced the idea that true fulfilment comes from not only personal achievements but also from empowering others to carve their own paths. This experience has undoubtedly become a cornerstone of my professional identity and will forever be a cherished memory in my personal and professional journey.

CAREER ADVICE

One thing I've learned is that true happiness comes from being brave enough to live authentically. When you dare to show your authentic self, you unlock a rare freedom that leads to genuine happiness. So, don't be afraid to take risks and follow your passions. Remember, the journey of self-discovery is not always easy, but it is incredibly rewarding. Surround yourself with supportive individuals who celebrate your uniqueness and encourage you to chase your passions without fear. This environment will nurture your bravery and allow you to thrive in your authenticity.

Remember, freedom is the key to happiness. Don't let others dictate how you should live your life. Take control and make decisions that align with your values and beliefs.

Additionally, don't shy away from vulnerability; it's a strength that fosters deeper connections with others. Embracing your flaws and imperfections not only makes you relatable but can also inspire those around you to do the same.

Ultimately, the secret to happiness lies in this freedom – freedom from judgement, from expectations, and most importantly, from being anything other than yourself. So, be brave, be unapologetically you, and watch as the world opens up to you in ways you never imagined!

CAYETANO RIVERA

SPANISH TORERO BULLFIGHTER

Cayetano is the son of Francisco Rivera 'Paquirri' and belongs to a long line of famous bullfighters: his great-grandfather was Cayetano Ordóñez, who fought under the name 'El Niño de la Palma', and was the inspiration for the young matador in Ernest Hemingway's novel The Sun Also Rises.

We didn't have a normal environment or surrounding growing up. I was born in Madrid but before I was one years old. We went to live in Sevilla, until my father died when I was 7 years old. Then we went back to Madrid until I was 14 years old and then I was sent to study abroad, in Switzerland. I did my military service after that and then I went to study in Los Angeles.

PASSION FOR BULLFIGHTING
I always wondered how powerful a feeling it would have to be in order to be willing to risk your life as a bullfighter. I'm fourth generation of bullfighters in my family, I wanted to know more about my roots, and to understand my history better, to feel what my ancestors felt. Now I know.

Curro Vazquez, a former bullfighter, has been my mentor, my master, my bullfighting manager.

LIFE AS A BULLFIGHTER
We like to consider it an art not a sport because it's an artistic form of expression. And yes I have had many dangerous calls.

It's a very risky profession. I can't forget the fact that my father died bullfighting when I was seven years old. Everything that happens in the bullfighting ring, it's real.

CAREER SUCCESS
It's very difficult to explain the mixture of feelings you experience fighting in the ring. But when you have a fulfilling bullfight at an important ring, I assure you there's nothing like it. But one can always improve. Excellence doesn't exist, so you just keep on learning.

My first bullfight was a great success although I had already "met" popularity before because of what my family had achieved as bullfighters before me.

CHALLENGES
Every bullfight it's a new challenge and it is extremely important to manage your fear, you have to learn to control your fear. I have also fought wounded. The way you fight defines the way you are.

ADVICE
In order to succeed as a bullfighter it will require a great amount of effort but the most important question they have to ask themselves is if they are willing to live or die for it..?

TRAINING
Once you already have the basic knowledge of bullfighting and strength, you will require about three months of training for a bullfight.

CAREER ADVICE
Unlike the rest of my colleagues I began bullfighting when I was 28 years old. I had the chance to

become a man before becoming a bullfighter. That gave me a good perspective of how I wanted things to be done, with whom and when.

MOTTO
Poem 'If', by Rudyard Kipling.

If you can keep your head when all about you
Are losing theirs and blaming it on you,
If you can trust yourself when all men doubt you,
But make allowance for their doubting too;
If you can wait and not be tired by waiting,
Or being lied about, don't deal in lies,
Or being hated, don't give way to hating,
And yet don't look too good, nor talk too wise:
If you can dream—and not make dreams your master;
If you can think—and not make thoughts your aim;
If you can meet with Triumph and Disaster
And treat those two impostors just the same;
If you can bear to hear the truth you've spoken
Twisted by knaves to make a trap for fools,
Or watch the things you gave your life to, broken,
And stoop and build 'em up with worn-out tools:
If you can make one heap of all your winnings
And risk it on one turn of pitch-and-toss,
And lose, and start again at your beginnings
And never breathe a word about your loss;
If you can force your heart and nerve and sinew
To serve your turn long after they are gone,
And so hold on when there is nothing in you
Except the Will which says to them: 'Hold on!'
If you can talk with crowds and keep your virtue,
Or walk with Kings—nor lose the common touch,
If neither foes nor loving friends can hurt you,
If all men count with you, but none too much;
If you can fill the unforgiving minute
With sixty seconds' worth of distance run,
Yours is the Earth and everything that's in it,
And—which is more—you'll be a Man, my son!

CAYETANO'S ADVICE

- *Study first.*

- *Train hard.*

- *Surround yourself with the best professionals but also good people.*

- *Look out for your money.*

GEORGES TOMB

AWARD-WINNING COMPOSER AND CONCERT PIANIST

Georges Tomb has had his works performed on prestigious stages worldwide, including the Venice Opera House. His compositions span classical music, ballet, and cinema, earning him accolades and comparisons to legendary figures such as Ennio Morricone.

Ever since I was a little boy, all my interests revolved around music. The piano was my first best friend, I could spend hours playing, exploring melodies, and expressing myself through it. Writing music came naturally to me, and I was always fascinated by watching my father orchestrate and compose. That world of harmony, structure, and emotion felt like home to me. Music wasn't just something I enjoyed; it was my passion, my language, and the way I connected with the world. From an early age, I knew that music would be my life's journey.

INSPIRATION

My Father's music was my greatest inspiration. He introduced me to the piano, which quickly became my closest companion, and guided me into the world of composition. But beyond just playing, he made me fascinated with the music behind the scenes.

I remember watching movies with him, and he would point out how music shaped the emotions of a scene.

That's when I truly realised the power of film scoring, the way a single melody could transform a moment on screen. I immersed myself in musicals, operas, and ballet, absorbing every note and every movement.

I knew I wanted my music to tell stories and convey powerful messages to the world. So, I followed that vision, studying, composing, and dedicating myself to the craft, until my passion became my profession.

CAREER TURNING POINT

My career has been a journey of continuous turning points, each opening a new chapter. My first major milestone in Europe, performing in Italy, was a defining moment. Collaborating with the San Remo Symphony and later with the Orchestra Filarmonica Italiana in Milan, where I was introduced on stage as the young Morricone, felt like stepping into a legacy I deeply admired.

Then came Carnegie Hall in 2024, where I premiered my piano concerto, A Memorial Bow, dedicated to Memorial Day. That performance was not just a highlight of my career but also a deeply emotional and artistic statement.

It feels like a lifetime of growth, yet every concert, every movie score, every performance has felt like a turning point. It's like climbing a ladder, step by step, until the world discovers more about my music. And with each step, I feel a greater responsibility to create, inspire, and leave a lasting impact through my work.

PASSION FOR CREATIVITY

It is not an easy industry, sharing your art with the world and hoping it resonates with others. As artists, we are deeply affected by the outside world, by life's circumstances, by personal experiences that can sometimes drain our creative energy. There were times when I felt disconnected from my music, where inspiration seemed distant, and exhaustion took over.

But I've learned that these moments are part of the journey. When I stepped away from music, even for a few days or weeks, I always found my way back, stronger, more inspired, and ready to create again. These phases weren't failures; they were resets, necessary breaks that allowed me to return with renewed passion.

The most important lesson I've learned is that an artist's first and biggest fan should be himself. If we don't believe in our craft, how can we expect others to? No matter how tough the journey gets, we must keep pushing forward, trusting in our art, and never giving up,because every challenge is just another step toward something greater.

ADVICE FOR SUCCESS

Success is not just about talent, it's about hunger, persistence, and unwavering belief in what you do. To truly make it, you have to be starving for your dreams, willing to push through obstacles, and never lose sight of your vision.

Persistence is key, never give up, no matter how difficult the journey gets. There will be moments of doubt, setbacks, and challenges, but those who succeed are the ones who keep going when others stop.

Above all, I believe in the magic I want to create in my work, an intangible force that fuels passion, creativity, and inspiration. Believing in that magic and working relentlessly hard to bring it to life is what separates true achievers from the rest. Hard work, passion, and resilience, those are the qualities that turn dreams into reality.

MUSICAL MENTOR

My father was my first musical mentor, being a composer himself, he introduced me to the world of music from an early age. Watching him compose, orchestrate, and bring music to life made me fall in love with the craft. He didn't |just teach me how to play or write music; he made me understand its depth, its storytelling power, and its emotional impact.

Over time, composing didn't feel like a choice, it felt naturally embedded in me. Music became my way of expressing myself, of shaping emotions, and of connecting with the world. It was as if every note I played was already a part of me, waiting to be written. That's when I knew that being a composer wasn't just what I wanted to do, it was who I was meant to be.

COMPOSER IN HOLLYWOOD

I have composed music for films in Hollywood, Europe, and Australia, including award-winning soundtracks such as *Enough*, *Lebanon's Darkest Hour*, *Inferno in Paris*, *Romano Artioli: Reviving Bugatti* and *Neenja*. These films have been recognised for their impact, and I am honoured that my compositions have contributed to their success.

CHALLENGES

A lot of challenges in my career, mainly the highly competitive nature of this industry. As a composer, it's not just about creating music, it's about getting it heard by the right people and ensuring it fits their vision and storytelling.

Music is deeply personal, and expressing our art in a way that resonates with others is not always easy.

THE FILM INDUSTRY

The film and music industry is particularly tough for composers like me because it requires more than just talent, it demands constant networking, adaptability, and persistence. Unlike other artistic fields, composers don't just create for themselves; we compose to serve a director's vision, an emotion, or a story. Finding the right projects, convincing people that our music is the right fit, and securing opportunities in an industry dominated by established names is a challenge in itself, being young as a composer was also a challenge.

Despite these obstacles, my passion for music has always pushed me forward. Every challenge is an opportunity to grow, refine my craft, and bring my music to new audiences worldwide.

INSPIRATION

I have been deeply inspired by both composers and filmmakers who have shaped the world of music and cinema. My father was my first and greatest mentor, introducing me to the beauty of composition. Musically, I have drawn inspiration from legends like Beethoven, Tchaikovsky, Morricone, Rota, John Williams, Brahms, Wagner, Scott Bradley, Verdi, and Mahler.

In film, visionaries like Steven Spielberg, Martin Scorsese, Christopher Nolan, & Alfred Hitchcock have profoundly influenced my understanding of storytelling and the role of music in cinema. Their ability to merge visuals with powerful scores has always fuelled my passion for composing. Each of these figures has played a role in shaping my artistic journey, pushing me to explore, innovate, and create music that tells stories and evokes deep emotions.

CAREER TURNING POINT

The first time I heard my music performed by an orchestra at a very young age. That moment made me realise the power of music and solidified my path as a composer.

ADVICE

Believe in your music, work relentlessly, and never give up.

This industry is tough, but magical.

SCOTT STEINDORFF

AMERICAN FILM PRODUCER

Scott Steindorff is an American film and television producer who specialises in adapting literary bestsellers into movies.

As a child, I was highly sensitive with high functioning autism, born with a unique operating system unequipped with standard features like logic and motor skills. Instead, my operating system came equipped with intensified sensitivity to feelings and empathy, possessing a heightened sense of smell, and sensitivity to colours and sounds. Fitting into the real world was challenging.

I grew up in the sixties. My father was a businessman and my mother was a nurse. We lived on a farm with horses and an acreage. I got into skiing at a young age and it became a passion until an injury forced me to stop competing. In school I became interested in theatre and performance which fuelled my passion for storytelling and film.

My family owned a large farm where I spent much of my time creating trails and riding horses. I just loved to be in nature.

At the age of four, I started skiing, which became a huge passion of mine. I most remember skiing and how I just loved being on the mountain.

CAREER BEGINNINGS

I was an imaginative kid so if I was imagining it, I was trying to write it or draw it. I was bullied and would escape it through creating imaginary worlds. Once in high school, I was involved in theatre. I got my start being in ski movies as a performer. It was then that I decided, early on, that I wanted to make movies.

CREATING FILMS

I have a great love for storytelling. I love how movies can make us feel. The human condition is about storytelling. We are constructed of stories. If I wasn't producing films, I would be writing books.

The best stories that can be produced into films are inspiring, life enhancing, and emotionally invoking. The stories that have an impact on the human condition.

I appreciate the fact that I'm able to tell stories and to write and produce television and movies. I think as we enter a new technological era, digital storytelling and short form content will transform lives. I want to be a part of it.

I face many challenges on set. First you have to define the problem and solve it and then move on to the next problem. It's usually best not to dwell on past problems because there are too many problems coming at you to focus on the past.

FIRST BIG BREAK

Writing a stage play for a 65 million musical at MGM Grand in Las Vegas called EFX show. There was essentially no director or producer so I had a lot of creative freedom and got to work closely with the star of the show to create it. It was a great learning experiences because once the show was up and running after a year, we could re-tool the show

based on audience reactions. It taught me about the importance of the audience in crafting stories.

BIGGEST SUCCESS
I'm working on that project right now.

INSPIRATION
I'm interested in the future and stories that evoke emotion. New, fresh, and original that we haven't seen before that are unique in nature.

YOUR MOST ENJOYED FILM
Empire Falls. I got to work with Paul Newman who is an amazing human being and artist.

INSPIRATION
Never giving up and being resilient to change. Overcoming difficulties because every human being must do so.

POWERHOUSE
Is to have confidence, self-esteem, self-worth and to believe in yourself.

SUCCESS TO YOU
Inspiring people.

SCOTT'S ADVICE

- *Always help others*
- *Never give up.*
- *Keep inspiring people.*

NOVLENE MILLS

WORLD CHAMPIONSHIP MEDALLIST | TRACK & FIELD ATHLETE

Novlene Mills is a four-time Olympic medallist and World Championship medallist. She is also a motivational speaker and breast cancer survivor.

BEGINNING
I grew up in Jamaica, St Ann; I am the seventh of my nine siblings. I grew up playing games on the street with other kids in the neighbourhood because my parents did not have much money to buy toys for us to play with. I did not start running track until my later years in high school. I was the first one out of my siblings to get a scholarship to go to college. I was excited because it was a chance for me that I knew my parents couldn't give me.

CAREER
In high school, I used to play netball, but a girl I know told the coach that I could run, and he asked me to join the track team. I did not for a year then I finally decided to. I started out running the 100m and 200m. I was not very good at it, but then, one day, he moved me to the 400m. I hated it but also found out I was much better in the 400m than the 100 and 200m.

After high school, I received a scholarship to college, but it was after I had transferred to the University of Florida that my coach, Tom Jones, really believed in me.

In 2003, I made the Jamaica World Championship Team to Paris, but I did not run. It was not until 2004, when I made the Olympic Team to Athens, that I started believing in myself. I got a bronze medal in the 4x400m relay, and ever since then, I've made national teams and also competed consistently internationally.

AMBITION
I haven't always been ambitious when it came to my track and field career. I started out wanting to be a teacher in high school. I did not even think making it to four Olympic Games or eight World Championships were even possible. I honestly grew up not thinking that being a professional athlete could be my career.

PASSION
In primary school I used to run a lot of sports carnivals. I knew I was faster than all the kids, and I just wanted to see how many trophies I could get at the end of the day.

CHALLENGES
In 2007, my college coach, who also coached me at the start of my professional career, passed away; it was a very devastating time because I was left without a coach in the middle of my season. In 2010, one of my sisters passed away, and I was in Berlin for a competition when I got the news. It was one of the most devastating days in my life. I flew home the next day without competing.

In 2012, I was diagnosed with breast cancer right before the Jamaica National Championship and the Olympic Games in London. My world turned upside down because I did not know why it was happening to me. After winning the Diamond League in 2014, my season was going through a very rough time. I was always tired and did not know why. I could not

finish a workout sometimes. I went to the doctor and found out I had a Thyroid infection. In 2016, while at the Olympic Games, I got a call from my mother, who had just been diagnosed with breast cancer.

Again, in 2016, while training for the 2017 season, my father had a stroke. There were many trying times that I had to deal with personally throughout my career.

TRAINING AND WINNING

I would be training five days per week. Winning the Diamond League felt really good. I came third at the Jamaican National. I knew they were my final races as I planned to retire at the end of the 2017 season. But it was good, as a couple of the Jamaican reporters picked someone else to win the race. I don't believe that they even had me in the top three to win in that event for the day.

2012 OLYMPICS

When I first found out about my breast cancer, I ran at the Jamaican national. I won, making my third Olympic team. But when I got back to Florida, I went to the doctor. They had me do the MRI scan, and I was already booked for a ticket to go to Paris. As much as it was so devastating to hear and prep for my surgery, my husband, Jameel Mills, encouraged me to go to Paris. He believed it would take my mind off what was actually happening. No one really knew about my cancer, only a handful of track friends.

BREAST CANCER TREATMENT

Two of my surgeries were in 2012, and one was three days after the Olympic Games. It was very challenging, especially when all my friends were back in training, and since no one knew what was going on with me, I was always making up excuses as to why I was not back at training. It was a really hard time, because I did not know what else to do.

PASSION

It's my greatest passion, sharing my story of perseverance and letting others know that no matter what they are going through, they don't have to give up; they can still rise to the top.

NOVLENE'S TIPS

- *Work hard, trust and believe in yourself. Keep people around in your circle who are going to push you and encourage you to work hard and do the right thing.*

- *Believe in your own ability. I am my biggest competitor.*

- *You have to be bold and hold your own. Be confident in whatever you do.*

- *Have hope: There is always light at the end of the tunnel. Continue to fight.*

PRINCESS JAHNAVI KUMARI MEWAR

FOUNDER AND HEAD OF PRIVATE EQUITY AUCTUS FORA

Princess Jahnavi has led her family office investment companies for the last decade. She has also founded and successfully launched several companies within the financial services, real estate, industrial and healthcare sectors.

I have always loved to be analytical/conduct analysis, even as a young child, of things consequential or otherwise. My interests evolved but never changed with age, location and life experiences. Economics was, is and will always remain a passion (not so much from purely an academic standpoint, but more pragmatic and application-based). Other areas of interest were the study of the human mind and nature, consciousness and Quantum Physics. Fashion and design have been a creative outlet for me in the past decade; prior to that, it was about appreciation, which has now led to hobby-based creation. Most recently, I have found terrific excitement from interior designing. My parents risked their new lake house by allowing me to handle it end-to-end; since then, it has become a hobby in which I find great delight.

After graduating from Deakin University, I received a placement with a consulting firm in Melbourne owned by my friend's father, where I had also interned during my last year of university. I continued working for my father's family office during this time. Eventually, I moved from consulting to the financial sector at Ord Minnett, a JP Morgan company, and finally left to set up my own boutique investment bank at the age of 25 in Melbourne.

So you could say I got my first start working for my father's investment company at sixteen.

LAUNCHING SEVERAL COMPANIES
The aforesaid was a natural progression and outcome of our private equity investment activities.

We use an investment methodology developed by me in 2011 – the ROM (Reverse Origination Methodology), allowing us to create assets as well as deploy capital subject to our in-house situational analysis.

EMPOWERING WOMEN
We incorporate an impact-centric capital deployment strategy within each of our portfolio assets and have found it to be much more consistent and sustainable in the long term. That's our first step towards creating a positive impact.

In the past few years, we have begun work on our Power of Policy platform, which is targeted not only towards empowering women but also addressing societal repair, geopolitical instability, the international investment landscape and the trust deficit prevailing across humanity at present.

I do believe that it is becoming easier for women to achieve such a role. I want to redefine as well as re-purpose the term "empowerment" and revitalise this critical movement to evoke a new sentiment: causing the women of this world to remember that in fact "power" resides in us. We already are the anchoring force to be reckoned with in life and at work.

TURNING POINT

There have been many, in terms of growing and evolving as a human being, finding a purpose beyond self-serving interests – this came in the form of my Power of Policy platform at the tail end of the second Covid lockdown.

This vision, in its infancy, was supported by my dearest friend Wendy Craft. Her unwavering love and friendship emboldened me to forge ahead.

CHALLENGES

When my boutique investment bank, JPM Capital, had just launched, I made the decision not to rely on family resources but only invest my own earnings from my previous job. Six months in, I had employees who were banking on salaries and with no revenue coming in, my own bank accounts grievously inching towards the red zone: the whole situation was fast turning into a feverish nightmare. May I humbly add that during this time, I didn't, however, feel any sense of defeat but only a heart-wrenching sense of responsibility towards my team?

They must not go without, was the last thought in mind each night before bed, and so I had a fire sale of several personal items (which might have included some of my very favourite pieces of clothing and shoes). In the end, just as the fire sale proceeds were depleting – we won an advisory mandate, then an M&A mandate, and so on.

INSPIRATION

I have always found inspiration from daily life, its interactions, and everyday experiences. If we pay attention, inspiration surrounds us – everyone we meet or work with, the experiences we have. The key is to be astutely observant and discerning in terms of where we should be inspired "to do" and when "not to do".

LEGACY

I would like to be remembered as someone who uplifted, which may be as small as engaging with a person and leaving them feeling happier.

JAHNAVI'S TIPS

- *Be authentic.*
- *Master your subject matter.*
- *Have foundational intellect.*

SUSIE WOLFF

FORMER PROFESSIONAL RACING DRIVER AND CURRENT MANAGING DIRECTOR OF F1 ACADEMY

Trailblazer: Susie Wolff is a Scottish former professional racing driver and current managing director of F1 Academy. Wolff started in karting before graduating to Formula Renault and Formula Three, then moving to the Deutsche Tourenwagen Masters to compete for Mercedes-Benz. In 2012 she was signed by the Williams F1 team as a development driver, making history at the 2014 British Grand Prix by becoming the first woman to take part in an F1 race weekend in 22 years.

You could say that motor sport was in my blood because my mum actually met my dad when she went to buy her first motorbike from his shop, and I got my first little go-kart at the age of eight. But at the age of eight, you're not thinking about a career, you're simply doing what you enjoy in the moment. And I had found something I loved doing. I was a very competitive little girl; I loved speed; I loved the adrenaline; I loved going to competitions. I found my passion so early in life and have a brilliant family who supported me on the journey.

INTEREST IN KARTING

It was my environment, and I was also in a very lucky position that I have a brother who's only 18 months older than me, so I was inspired by him. My parents were always treating us as equals, never differentiating between son and daughter. And that's something I really appreciate now, because I never realised I was doing something unusual for a girl.

A CAREER IN MOTOR SPORT

It was very much a hobby and not something that I saw as a career, despite it being very competitive, until the age of 13, when I was taken to watch the Formula 3 race. That's when the goal was born in my head that I wanted to be a Formula 1 driver. I realised that you could make a career out of being a racing driver.

FIRST WOMAN TO TAKE PART IN THE BRITISH GRAND PRIX

It was a huge amount of preparation to get ready for the test. I was doing a lot of the development and simulator work in the background, but there was pressure because people were interested to find out whether I would be quick enough, whether a woman would be strong enough to drive a modern-day Formula 1 car. And obviously, it's such a male-dominated sport that my driving caused a lot of media attention. But despite the pressure, I will always be grateful to have had the opportunity and taking to the track as a British driver in a British team like Williams at the British Grand Prix was definitely the highlight of my career and a very special moment.

The team gave me a lot of support and I knew I had to be well prepared. It was my one chance to show what I could do. But of course, I also had a lot of detractors, who didn't think I would be quick enough: who didn't think I would be strong enough.

But for me, you can never keep everyone happy. I don't worry about everyone else's opinion, because if you don't believe in yourself, you can't expect others to believe in you.

CHANGING THE GAME FOR WOMEN IN SPORT

Well, I never set out to change the world of motor sport for women. I was simply a young girl who found her passion and, still to this day, I love being on a racetrack, whether that's karting or Formula 1. The journey has, at times, been very lonely and, at

times, been very tough. But I think for any athlete to get to the top of any sport, it is tough.

And now in my new role, it gives me a lot of satisfaction to know that I'm giving back, that I'm helping the next generation and creating a platform which can drive impactful and positive change by giving young women more opportunities and support to excel both on track and off track.

It's hugely competitive in motor sport and obviously quite challenging in that you need financial backing to compete at the highest levels. This financial barrier has always been a tough one for any driver, male or female, to navigate. You need to find sponsorship. In F1 Academy, we give the young female drivers a lot of track time and support, with them only needing to bring a vastly reduced financial contribution. So, we're really levelling the playing field and giving them the best chance at going on to success.

AWARDED AN MBE
It was a great honour, but I'm not doing what I'm doing to win awards or to get accolades or recognition. I'm doing it because it's a passion. I want the next generation not to make the same mistakes I did and to learn from all my experience.

I'm a big believer that in life it's all about give and take, and you need to give back.

CHALLENGES
Everyone says you need to make failure your friend because failure is such an important part of the journey. I definitely think it's an important part of the journey, but it has never been my friend, even to this day. I hate defeat. I hate failure. It leaves a knot in my stomach when there's something I haven't achieved, and I'm someone who's normally very goal-focused and hugely determined. But of course, there have been many times in my life where I've had to cope with big failures. I've definitely lost a lot more races than I've ever won, but I think that the resilience to pick yourself back up and keep going is what differentiates those who make it and those who don't. I believe it's one of the most important character traits for anyone who wants to succeed in a very competitive environment.

Just don't give up.

RESILIENCE
A lot of my strength comes from my childhood because I started racing at an early age. I had parents who always taught me the value of hard work and never to give up. And that's something which, even in the business world, I remember every day. When I had the idea to get the 10 Formula 1 teams to support a car and driver, meaning that for the first time in the history of the sport, they would be giving their name and livery to something outside of F1, so many people told me it would be impossible; but we did it. And sometimes, the impossible is possible.

FINDING SUCCESS
I think it's sometimes quite difficult to define what success is because for me, as I've got older, I've definitely understood that success is having a contentment and happiness in your life and not everyone is competitive, not everyone is ambitious, and it's about living your life how you want to live it and not allowing others to put pressure on what their expectations are or what their beliefs are. Only you know what makes you truly happy, and it's about finding that passion in your life, whatever it may be.

But knowing that your own personal happiness and contentment is what defines success in your life. It's not how many awards you've won, it's not how much money you earn, how many material assets you have. I think it really comes down to being content.

INSPIRATION
Definitely my parents. They gave me such a great start in life. And I had a wonderful role model in my mother and both my grandmothers and, obviously then, my husband, but many other people who have helped me on the journey. And I think it's really important to surround yourself with good people, people who are willing to tell you when you've not done something right or when you need to improve and not wrap you in cotton wool. And I'm certainly very lucky to have a lot of good people around me, particularly my family and husband.

FUTURE ASPIRATIONS
I want to make sure F1 Academy has a solid foundation to go on and flourish middle to long term,

because I think we have the chance to make a huge impact in the world of motor sport and change it for the better in terms of diversity. We can inspire the next generation to see that motor sport is no longer a man's world. But we've got to get it right, this is a once in a lifetime chance.

LEGACY
I don't think too much about legacy. I try to live in the moment, but I hope that I can be remembered as someone who opened the door and inspired other women to see that there are opportunities in the world of motor sport and, most importantly, that it's not just a man's world anymore.

SUSIE'S TIPS

- *Define in which area you want to work and where your passion lies, because it's much easier to find success in something you really enjoy doing because it makes the difficult days much easier to cope with.*

- *Believe in yourself. If you can't believe in yourself, don't expect others to believe in you.*

- *Don't be scared to speak up when you need to have your voice heard. It doesn't mean you need to be overbearing and talk all the time, but make sure when you've got something important to say that you stand up and let yourself be heard.*

- *Have a lot of determination and tenacity. There can be moments that are very tough, but you just have to keep going and fight for where you want to get to and what your goals are.*

YOU CAN MANIFEST ANYTHING YOU WANT IN LIFE THROUGH VISION, HARD WORK, PASSION AND DETERMINATION.

STEPH ADAMS

SHARLETTE HAMBRICK

EMMY AWARD-WINNING NEWS AND ENTERTAINMENT PRODUCER

Sharlette Hambrick is the CEO of Y-Tulip Productions, where she serves as the president of development and production. She is also a Director on the Hollywood Foreign Press Association Board.

My childhood consisted of reading, long walks with friends and church. Reading was my escape from three brothers; the long walks were encouraged to the beautiful landscape and parks in Washington DC. This is where I grew up, and church came from my mother's dedication to religion. I was a good student and social in school; some may say too social. I had the frequent reprimand for talking too much in class. We can now call it communication skills.

CAREER

A Communication/English instructor at my high school named Ms Webb encouraged me to pursue journalism. Ms Webb suggested I enter a summer course at Howard University between my junior and senior year of high school. This course leads to an internship at WHUR Radio station in the News Department at the University. I knew then that I would be a Broadcast/Journalism student in College. I attended Pepperdine University in Malibu to follow that dream, which many in my community thought must be out of reach. Once I completed university, I returned home to Washington, DC. I first managed to secure a part-time job at the local TV station WRC-TV while serving as a sales clerk and personal shopper at Saks Fifth Avenue. The latter, of course, helped with my wardrobe concerns required after four years in Malibu, California. My next promotion was to NBC network news, which included *The Today Show*, *Meet the Press* and *Nightly News*.

SUCCESS IN TV

The turning point to my success was long hours and consistently volunteering for every show on NBC. This contributed to my hard news burnout. Around this time, I had the luck of meeting a kind and funny comedian named Eddie Murphy, who was on tour with his show. This is what opened my ambitions to Hollywood, CA. Rockets went off, and I loaded up my VW Jetta and headed for Hollywood with my dear friend Nina.

Kim joined, and we enjoyed success in entertainment in our twenties. I got a job at *Entertainment Tonight* on the Paramount Studio lot. This would be the start of a second career and my most rewarding one.

OVERCOMING DEFEAT

My deepest sense of failure came when I left CBS/Paramount and *Entertainment Tonight*/*The Insider*. I had given most of my adult life to this brand. This was who I believed myself to be: Sharlette Hambrick, Senior Producer, *ET*. I was a single mom, with a 10-year-old child. I trusted and believed I would be there until my darling entered college.

My mother was not well, my brother passed away, and my relationship of 10 years with my boyfriend ended. I could not share all of this with anyone with the expertise to get me through it. Who wants to admit ageism? My friends were there as always. My darling friend Nevbahar invited me to Turkey for a few weeks to try to lift the depression. I am sure she knew I was not myself. Then, negotiations for my next career move fell through. My child and I survived.

QUALITIES FOR SUCCESS

I think a rewarding quality would be to truly make other people's lives better. Hearing a laugh from someone or, just for me, the excitement of remembering a person's name or face instantly. Making sure individuals feel seen and heard. I also think you must be able to put trust in others and allow them to contribute to their lives. We have all lost trust in a colleague, friend and or family member at some point. You cannot be frozen by this experience. View your blessed success as an opportunity to be generous.

EMMY AWARD

This Emmy Award acknowledgement was bittersweet. The year I received the Emmy was my last year at *ET*. I was proud and thankful. I always think about all those wonderful people who had passed through *Entertainment Tonight* and did not have that opportunity to receive the famous statue.

I share it with them. They deserve it as well.

INSPIRATION

I am inspired by women celebrating women. My inspiration comes from the rapid changes in my industry: the progression from network stations and syndication to cable and on to streaming; from standard entertainment experiences to VR and AI. My inspiration comes from major studio films to independent films. I even get inspiration from Instagram, TikTok and Meta.

WORKING WITH THE GOLDEN GLOBES

I served as an Independent Executive Board Director of the Hollywood Foreign Press Association, HFPA. The HFPA, a group of immigrant entertainment journalists, created the Golden Globes. They were going through some game-changing difficulties that needed immediate attention.

I thought I could be of strategic service in helping to both save the brand of the Golden Globes and the philanthropic achievements as well. I also enjoyed researching and contacting Black entertainment writers around the world and inviting those who qualified to join as voters of the Golden Globes. I looked forward to the show, and many in Hollywood benefited from the 81-year-old institution, including myself. I was honoured and elated to see the success and preservation of both the Golden Globes brand and the GG Philanthropic Foundation this year. I wish them much success.

PASSION

I am passionate about Skye, my spectacular, kind and talented child. I am obsessed with audiobooks. I still love long walks amongst the trees and the sound of the ocean. I enjoy the cuisine of my birthplace, New Orleans, LA. I am passionate about old friends and new friends around the world. I adore Turkey, smiling children and yellow tulips. I will always embrace an excellent film.

ASPIRATIONS

To have the wisdom and means to be as generous as I can. I aspire to serve on more boards in which I can make a difference. I also secretly aspire to run a film festival for a few years. Riding in the bush of Botswana on a strong horse again. Stargazing from a boat in the South of Turkey and Istanbul. Snow angels with Skye.

I will be finishing my book in hopes that it will be adapted into a comedy/drama series. I hope the project will bring both laughter and inspiration. A complete wardrobe makeover and a minimalistic life.

WHO IS WHO INTERNATIONAL AWARD 2023

This was a highlight in my life. Actually, Prince Nereides de Bourbon received an extremely prestigious award the year prior. I was nominated for the 'World Woman Leader of Global Entertainment & Racial Equality – Who is Who International Award 2023'. I was ecstatic when I was told I would be honoured by him. The warm reception from the charming Prince Nereides de Bourbon and Lello Ammirati was unforgettable. The founders, Dimitrios Goris and his delightful wife, Vicky Papageorgopoulou, were a joy. Athens is a star. I cannot wait to be back.

SHARLETTE'S TIPS

- *I cannot say there is any one way to accomplish a chosen goal. If you want to be a journalist, it is expected that you would have attended college. That would be the start. That would be the best environment to explore many possibilities.*

- *Writers should just write. (I am not a strong writer. This is why I veered towards producing.)*

- *If you have an idea – register it first and then research the appropriate leaders you should share your ideas with. Narrow your scope, only to broaden when required.*

- *Do not be frightened to request an internship or a mentorship.*

ROSANNA SCOTTO

HOST OF "GOOD DAY NEW YORK" ON FOX 5

As a young child, I was always interested in TV news. We watched the evening news as we were eating dinner. At that time, there were very few women covering news and so, when they did appear, it really caught my attention and spurred my interest in that profession.

While I was in college, I had several internships at ABC News. When I graduated from Catholic University, I got a low-entry position at Ted Turner's TV station in Atlanta. I started working for the evening news as a chyron operator, and over time, I worked my way up as a researcher, field producer, and reporter. At the time, we nicknamed the TV station the Turner 'School of Broadcasting'. It seemed like they hired everybody who just graduated college. It was a wonderful experience to really learn the ins and outs of the TV business.

After spending a few years in Atlanta, I moved back to work on a local morning TV show with Regis Philbin and Cindy Garvey in NYC. I did some producing for Regis as well as reporting. He was a wonderful mentor and a great friend. From there, I was hired at *Eyewitness News* as a general assignment reporter. I stayed there for about three years and made my way over to FOX Five. I was hired as a reporter, and many years later, I was given the opportunity to anchor the 10PM news. I've since invested in a new alarm clock because, for the last 10 years, I have anchored *Good Day New York*. It has been a wonderful experience to interview newsmakers and celebrities.

THE CHALLENGES

As a native New Yorker, covering the terrorist attacks in New York City was extremely challenging. It was emotional to go down to the World Trade Center and report on the lives lost and the devastation to our city. I lost many friends in the attack. I will never forget when one of my neighbours came to my apartment the next day and told me about her last conversation with her brother, who died inside the World Trade Center. There were days when I cried on the air during my reports. The rules for covering a news event are changed.

BEING IN THE SPOTLIGHT

Covering the Woody Allen and Mia Farrow custody battle catapulted my reports onto an international stage. I was exclusively given the videotape that Mia took of her daughter Dylan talking about what Woody allegedly did to her. The person who slipped us the tape was not friends with either one of them. He was concerned that because of their celebrity, Dylan would not get the help she needed. We never showed the tape on the air but I did go on TV and explain what I saw and heard. From that moment on, we had many exclusive reports, which were all picked up by international outlets regularly.

I am so grateful to have a front-row seat to history. At the end of the day, though, it boils down to family. As many working moms know, it's not easy to raise a family and have a career. While the juggling hasn't always been perfect, my husband and children know they are always my priority.

Finding that family/work balance is what I am most proud of.

GIVING BACK

I have been involved with a number of charities, including HeartShare Human Services. I am Brooklyn born and raised. This organisation is based in Brooklyn and is passionate about nurturing and empowering children and adults facing challenges. I serve on their board and know their focus is to make

a difference. Judging from the families I speak to, they are a game changer.

SOCIAL MEDIA
I now understand the importance of social media. I regularly live tweet during our three-hour broadcast in the morning. It gives me a chance to interact with our audience and find out what is on their mind. It is also an opportunity to show a personal side.

THE SIDE HUSTLE
For years, TV journalists have been one-dimensional. These days, the people who watch us also want to know who we really are. I love the fact that I'm able to share some of my passions. My family and I own Fresco by Scotto restaurant in midtown Manhattan. It's a wonderful opportunity to share recipes and my love of family. I believe it has helped my credibility as a TV journalist.

FEMALE EMPOWERMENT
It's great to see some of the positive changes in the business world.

Hopefully, the young women who are following in my footsteps will have an easier time navigating the business while raising a family.

One of my first mentors in the business was Rosanne Scarmadella. She was one of the first Italian-American women on the air in local TV news. She was very helpful in showing me the ropes and introducing me to people in the business.

BEING A POWERHOUSE WOMAN
I am humbled to be included in an incredible group of women! I didn't set out to change the status quo. I wanted a seat at the table. I wanted a chance to report on the big stories! And I wanted to do it from the perspective of a woman.

ROSANNA'S ADVICE
* Cultivate contacts. You need to find a nugget of information no one else has.
* Work harder! This business requires you to work nights, early mornings, weekends and holidays!
* Build your social media. News Directors check to see if you have a following and what you're posting.

ROSANNA'S MOTTO
Keep learning and reinventing! Staying in the status quo is death.

DELPHINE JELK

PERFUMER FOR GUERLAIN

A leader in the world of fragrances, Delphine Jelk is the creator of Guerlain's haute perfumery collections, where some perfumes have cost over $135,000 and above.

I grew up in Switzerland in a quiet town with two brothers and one sister. I'm the eldest. My childhood was very sweet and happy until I lived a drama that changed my life forever. When I had my degree, I left Switzerland to go to Paris for my studies. I loved this feeling of freedom to be anonymous in a big city. Everything was new and so exciting.

CAREER BEGINNINGS

I started by studying fashion design in Paris at ESMOD International. To get my diploma, I had to create a clothing collection. I chose men's home wear using ivory cashmere and beige linen. I wanted to express those fabrics and colours actively. A fragrance supplier helped me to create two fragrances inspired by my collection. I loved this experience so much, it was a revelation. I decided to continue my studies in the fragrance world, going to the Grasse Institute of Perfumery in the South of France. A bespoke fragrance is an amazing journey.

We first meet in Guerlain's lab in Paris and talk about who you are, where you are coming from, about your active memories, and then we start creating your fragrance together.

It will take months, but at the end, it will be your scent forever. You can also choose to transmit it to your children or to someone of your choice.

I remember a woman who had six daughters. She needed her perfume to please the six of them because she wanted them to wear her fragrance after her death. Her husband had to like it as well. It was an incredible experience. Some of these perfumes can take over eight months to create.

INSPIRATION

Sometimes, my inspiration comes from art, fashion, a movie, a colour, a person, travel, a raw material, but before anything, it comes from an emotion that I translate effectively.

I have always had a very strong imagination, like a bubble of dreams that would make me happy. It has always inspired me a lot. Today, it's my intuition

that inspires me and my loved ones, because love makes you happy and happiness makes you creative. That's how it works for me.

CHALLENGES
I missed my first perfumer's job because I was a girl. This man told me he preferred to hire a guy; girls were too complicated. I was so disappointed and frustrated, I understood at this moment that being a woman makes it more difficult professionally.

QUALITIES FOR SUCCESS
Believe in your dreams and never give up. I didn't just want to become a perfumer, I over-wanted it! I believe in the 3P theory of perfume, which is: passion, patience and perseverance.

FUTURE ASPIRATIONS
I have a dream job being Guerlain's Creative Director for fragrances and a loving family with my four children. I feel so lucky and grateful.

I used to project myself into the future all the time. Now I try to live as much as possible in the present and to live in full awareness and enjoy my life.

LEGACY
That I always believe in my dreams, I never give up. Also, I'm caring and kind; this is so important to me.

DELPHINE'S ADVICE

- *Be passionate.*

- *Work hard.*

- *Be audacious.*

- *Accept that it takes time.*

TATIANA BLATNIK

ENTREPRENEUR, FOUNDER OF BREATHE

Tatiana Blatnik has dedicated her career creating partnerships for social impact. Guided by her passion for giving a voice to others, heritage-based projects and a holistic approach to healthy living.

I have always been drawn to human connection, storytelling, social impact, health and healing. As a child I spent most of my time in the kitchen, learning to cook, using food as a way of connecting the family to bring people together and also as a way of connecting my own roots and identity. Food was my identity for a long time as we moved around. It tied my Venezuelan heritage with my mother's Spanish upbringing and German roots and the list goes on. I was blessed to have been brought up by someone that knew about healing through herbs and this ancestral knowledge stayed with me. It has continued to stay with me. I also love to help others, leading community service and through various bake sales.

I decided to study Sociology at Georgetown University as people, patterns and building healthier communities is a topic that fascinated me.

From a young age, I have also loved acting. I was very interested in identifying the tools that people use to find strength through adversity. That curiosity, along with a deep love for travelling and getting to know different people and places in the world has shaped and defined my path toward wellness.

THE BEGINNING OF BREATHE

Breathe wasn't born from a single moment—it was a series of experiences, realisations and a core part of my personal story. After losing my father to suicide, I saw first-hand how stigma can keep people from seeking help. This fuels our mission and drives our goal at Breathe: to raise awareness, promote self-care and ensure mental health resources are accessible to all. We have been able to reach individuals and families who need it most.

Breathe was created to ensure that no one feels alone in their struggles and that mental well-being is treated as a priority, not a privilege. A central element of our work and one of our proudest milestones is our partnership with the Kevin Love Fund (KLF) in the US. Established by NBA Champion and Olympic Gold medallist Kevin Love, after experiencing a public panic attack, the Kevin Love Fund is committed to equipping young people and educators with the tools to develop emotional resilience. Their Social Emotional Learning (SEL) curriculum, which we are now scaling globally together, has already impacted over 100,000 children and adolescents across more than twenty countries, demonstrating the powerful effect of comprehensive mental health education.

I am very proud of this initiative and what makes our partnership even more significant to me is that both our organisations are women-led, adding an extra layer of meaning, grace and boldness to our collaboration.

At Breathe, we are honoured to have the auspices of the Greek Ministry of Health, the Greek Ministry of Education and Ministry of Sports, The Hellenic Olympic Committee, working closely with the World Health Organisation – our global partners, the Stavros Niarchos Foundation, The Hellenic Initiative, the Stelios Haji-Ioannou Foundation, The Petrocheilos Foundation and the Maria Tsakos Public Benefit Foundation.

GREECE AND ITS HERITAGE

Greece is a place of beauty, history and resilience, but what brings me the most joy is the sense of community. Whether on an island surrounded by the deep blue sea or in the heart of Athens, there is a warmth and generosity here that is truly special. Having travelled the world, I can say that only in Greece can one really feel this sense of *filoxenia* (hospitality).

I believe that Greece has the potential to lead a global shift in how we define well-being—not just as the absence of illness, but as a holistic way of life. Right now, my focus is on driving investments that align with this vision through my private company. We are at a defining moment in time where the world is actively seeking new models for health, longevity and mental resilience. Greece is uniquely positioned to be at the forefront of this movement. Through my platform, I invite visionary investors, innovators and organisations that are committed to creating legacy.

CHALLENGES

I've often had to trust my intuition and go against the odds, even when it wasn't the easiest route. As all people who have their own companies, there have been moments of doubt, but each step forward, even the small ones, have been worth it.

I will say that one of the biggest challenges has been breaking the stigma around mental health, which requires team effort and societal support. There is still hesitation in talking about mental health openly. But with every new partnership, every campaign, we are changing that. Another challenge has been navigating systemic barriers—creating real change requires persistence and there is no short cut to impact.

INSPIRATION

Collaboration, bringing together leaders across health, hospitality and wellness to create impactful projects is what drives me. Whether it's building partnerships, integrating well-being into hospitality, enabling mental health access or fostering environments where people thrive. The power of collective impact is undeniable.

I am inspired by people, seeing someone find their voice, reach out for help or share their story gives me hope. Our flagship initiative at Breathe, the Uniform of Hope campaign, where twenty eight Greek Olympians came together to advocate for mental health, was a moment that reaffirmed why this work matters. Strength is not about never struggling—it's about having the courage to ask for help when you need it most.

QUALITIES FOR SUCCESS

Authenticity, resilience and the ability to lift others as they rise. True power isn't about individual success—it's about using your influence to create a ripple effect.

LEARNING THROUGH CHALLENGES

There have been moments when I felt overwhelmed—times when change felt too slow or challenges felt insurmountable.

But I've learned that failure is not the opposite of success; it's part of the journey. I remind myself that progress, no matter how small, is still progress. And I lean on my support system—they are my greatest source of strength.

LESSONS SINCE STARTING BREATHE

1. Partnerships create Impact
2. Change takes time but every step forward counts
3. Trust your intuition

POWER OF RESILIENCE

My mother has had one of the most profound influences in my life. Her resilience and strength in raising my brother and myself, taught me the power of resilience in the most genuine form possible and for that I am forever grateful.

My mother has an incredible ability to face adversity with grace and optimism, always pushing forward and turning obstacles into opportunities. Her unique blend of elegance, determination (and her effortless style!) has shaped not just my values but also the way I approach challenges in my own life and work. She also reminds me to dance, laugh and enjoy life!

CAREER SUCCESS

On the professional front, I have been inspired by entrepreneurs, philanthropists and people I have met along my journey of life: from CEOs and founders to yoga teachers, holistic healers, chefs and artists who have transformed personal struggles into opportunities for growth and impact.

Many of these individuals turned their challenges into a driving force for creating solutions that make a real difference in people's lives, scaling their business and transforming communities.

Carole Bamford, founder of Daylesford Organic, had a vision for healthier, sustainable food and created a thriving business that has created a real impact, transforming communities and also inspiring others to follow suit.

I have also been inspired by athletes, artists and leaders who use their platform to speak openly, unite people and make positive, sustainable impact. I have to say that I have deep respect for Novak Djokovic for his holistic approach to excellence — combining rigorous physical training with a focused, resilient mindset and his inspiring commitment to nurturing both body and mind, equally.

Nobu Matsuhisa, who followed his passion for Japanese cuisine and created his Nobu empire through perseverance, creativity and ability to innovate. What we see is the success – it is the story behind the success – the failures as we call it, and his never giving up that made him a success – and that is what I admire.

DEFINING MOMENT

Seeing an idea turn into a movement that reaches thousands of people is something I will always be proud of.

TATIANA'S ADVICE

- *Trust the process and be patient.*

- *Learn to say no.*

- *Surround yourself with people that lift you up.*

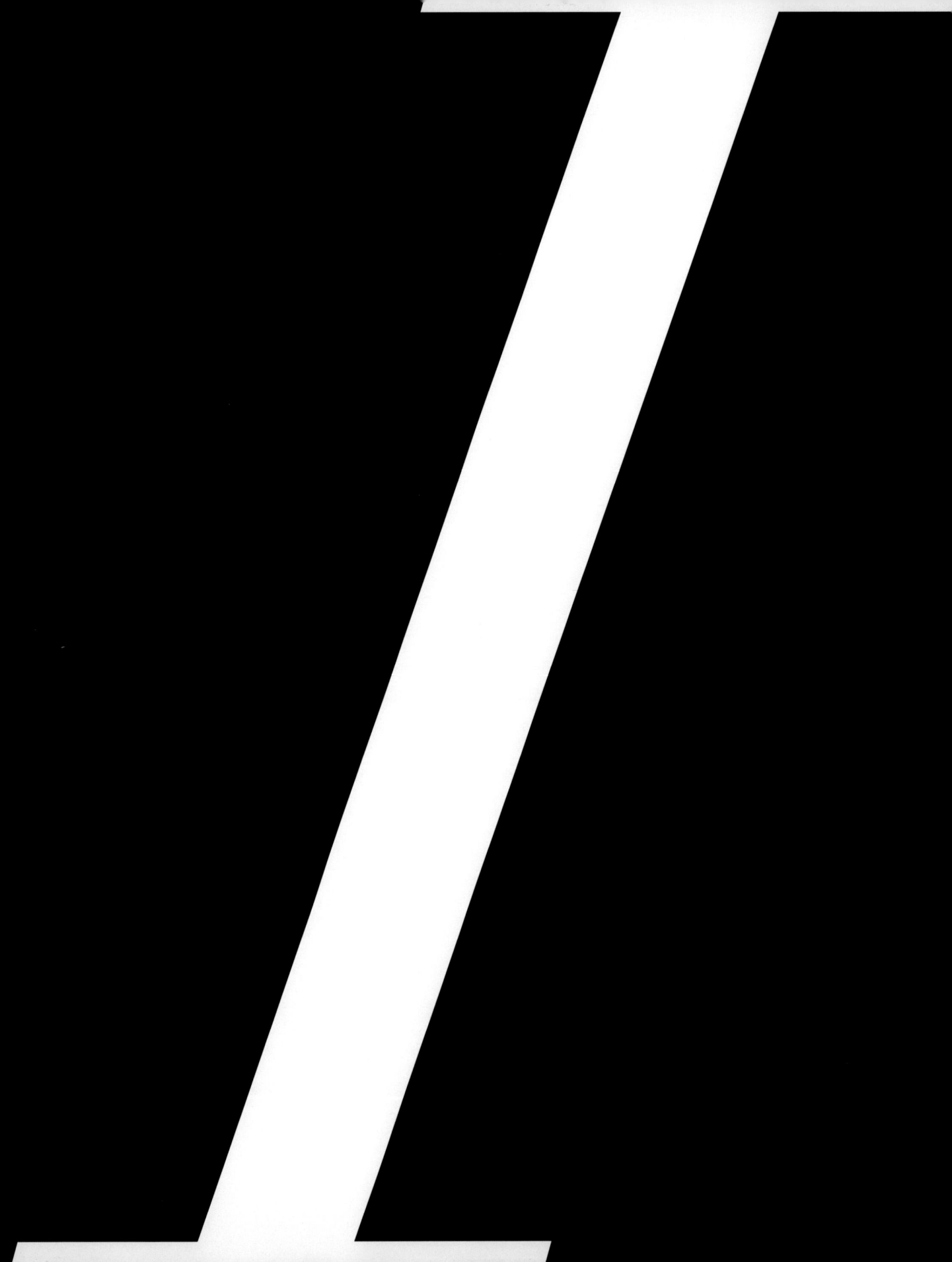

*I NEVER DREAMED
ABOUT SUCCESS,
I WORKED FOR IT.*

ESTÉE LAUDER

NADINE MIRADA

SUPERMODEL AND GUESS MODEL

A true icon: Nadine Mirada is the first Austrian curve model who made it in America, shining on billboards on Rodeo Drive and next to the Mirage in Las Vegas. She has her own TV show, Glam, *and created her own market and established curvy women as models in Austria.*

From the very beginning, I was a typical girl, playing princess and loved to dress up. I was in front of the camera for the first time at three years old. But as I got older, the industry just wasn't very open to or accepting of healthy, natural curves. But I am really happy that the mentality of the industry has changed, and I believe that my time is now.

Even though I might be a bit older than most models, I am happy that I took the time to get a good education and develop my personality…both of which are really invaluable qualities to me.

BUILDING THE BRAND

My career started on Instagram. No agency wanted to sign me, so I used social media to attract potential clients. Because I never conformed to standard measurements and never wanted to adapt, it was important for me to stay true to myself, follow my own path, and achieve my goals. It took me a bit longer to get to California than I would have planned, but I am so thankful that I've stayed true to myself and my body. I am really proud of the woman I have become and am really in tune with who I am, both physically and mentally. I love my body and I feel good in it – no one can take that away from me.

I found out that if I want to shine glamorously on the outside, I have to feel happy and self-confident on the inside.

Additionally, I've learned the importance of remaining true to myself as well as treating others and myself with complete respect and send the love I want to get back.

BEING A GUESS MODEL

It's truly a dream come true. I have always loved Guess, so I posted a picture of me wearing a Guess outfit on my Instagram account, and I tagged the brand and Paul Marciano in the picture. I caught their attention, and we connected for a test shoot when I was in Los Angeles for the Oscars. It's quite a "simple" story, but that's exactly how it happened. It was really such an incredible experience. From the professionalism to the attention to detail, I felt completely in my element.

Guess is truly a unique brand, and I felt that we vibed really well together. I am really proud of the outcome. Every single Guess/Marciano campaign was unique and special. I believe one never gets used to seeing oneself in larger-than-life images at the most famous places in the world, from my hometown in Vienna to Las Vegas.

CAREER HIGHLIGHT

When Paul Marciano discovered me, it was no coincidence. I always saw myself as a Guess model and wore their clothing, tagging them on Instagram until the company and the CEO took notice. At that time, I was invited to the Oscars in Hollywood, Los Angeles, as a blogger.

CHALLENGES

Over many years, there was a significant challenge in the modelling industry as it was unwilling to include models in their roster who didn't conform to the standard measurements of 90-60-90. After numerous

applications to agencies, this proved to be a continuous setback. However, ultimately, this period of adversity served as motivation for my personal growth. I learned to navigate setbacks and not let them discourage me.

Instead of being disheartened by rejections, I recognised my uniqueness and individuality as strengths. This experience inspired me to forge my own path and not conform to unrealistic standards.

Over time, I realised that true beauty lies in diversity and individuality. I created my own opportunities by utilising social media and reaching out directly to potential clients. This persistence and self-belief ultimately led to my success, and I emerged stronger from these challenges.

INSPIRATION
My mom. She's my heart and soul and my greatest support.

PASSIONS
I am most passionate about my family and friends, cherishing the deep connections and shared moments with them. My work is another significant source of passion, as I find fulfilment and purpose in what I do. Travelling holds a special place in my heart, allowing me to explore new cultures and broaden my perspective. Additionally, I have a keen interest in shopping, finding joy in discovering unique items and expressing my personal style. Each of these aspects contributes to a well-rounded and fulfilling life for me.

SELF CARE
I lead a very healthy lifestyle. I consistently go to bed before midnight, rarely consume alcohol, don't smoke, and maintain a nutritious diet. Additionally, I engage in regular physical activity. These habits contribute not only to my physical well-being but also serve as a crucial foundation for mental balance.

I place particular emphasis on "Me Time" and self-care. In a profession often marked by demanding and stressful routines, like the modelling industry, I consider these moments essential. Focusing on my personal needs and well-being is a vital counterbalance.

NADINE'S TIPS

- *Always shine twice and be authentic and unique!*

- *Set goals and focus on them.*

- *Sometimes, you don't have to do certain things to ultimately be successful.*

- *If you radiate glamour, you will shine in the end!*

LAUREN BUSH

CEO AND CO-FOUNDER OF FEED PROJECTS

GROWING UP
I was born in Denver, Colorado and moved to Houston, Texas, when I was eight years old. I have two younger siblings, Pierce and Ashley.

ENTERING THE FASHION INDUSTRY
I started modelling when I was in high school and continued very part-time through college. It was a fun experience getting to go to New York and learn more about the fashion industry, but ultimately it was not what I wanted to do as a career.

STARTING A FASHION LABEL
I started my own label, Lauren Pierce, in 2009 with the mission to use only eco-friendly and artisan-made fabrics. It was very specialised, working with women in Cambodia hand-weaving silks and with a group hand-dyeing fabric in the DRC. It was sold exclusively at Barneys for several years and then later at Calypso.

STARTING FEED
I was inspired to start FEED right out of college. As a student, I had the opportunity to travel around the world as an Honorary Student Spokesperson for the UN World Food Programme to learn about and witness first-hand the realities of poverty and hunger that approximately 800 million people face around the world. I was very moved, in particular, by the School Meal programs, which are helping get kids the food and nutrition they need using a free school meal, which simultaneously encourages education, especially for young girls. I started FEED in 2007 as an impact-driven lifestyle brand that gives consumers a tangible and shareable way to participate in our mission, which is to end worldwide childhood hunger by providing school meals with every single purchase.

CHALLENGES
When I started FEED as a social business, I did not know what a give-back business model like ours entailed. It was a relatively new idea at the time, so I didn't have many examples to look to, and thus a lot of retailers and customers did not know what to make of us. Also, figuring out how to balance being a very philanthropic business, while also growing as a company, has been a core challenge.

We have managed to lead with mission and heart, while also growing our business. I think it is also admitting what you don't know and surrounding yourself with people that bring new expertise and ideas to the table. I am lucky to have had an amazing support system of teammates and advisors over the years that have helped me shape and grow FEED.

BALANCING FAMILY
Being a working mum is not always easy, but I am lucky to have a job I feel passionate about, as well as kids who seem to accept the fact that their mama works.

MOTTO
The Golden Rule – 'Treat others as you would want to be treated.'

CHARLOTTE TILBURY

MAKEUP ARTIST AND FOUNDER OF CHARLOTTE TILBURY

An icon in the beauty industry, Charlotte Tilbury is responsible for some of our favourite red carpet looks on the world's most celebrated women. A makeup artist for more than twenty years, her passion for transforming faces has resulted in the creation of her cult beauty line, sharing her makeup secrets and enabling every woman to have access to her makeup and beauty secrets.

From the very beginning, I've worked in the beauty industry. I have always believed in the magic and power of makeup ever since I was a little girl. I understood the power of makeup for myself when I first applied mascara aged 13 and instantly felt more empowered, confident and noticed. I've always been fascinated by the power a beautiful woman has when she enters a room, and I wanted to understand that type of beauty and how its magnetic pull can command attention. I would study women's iconic faces obsessively to understand their beauty DNA. I taught myself how I could morph and cheat features to be bigger and brighter! A real turning point for me was meeting Mary Greenwell, aged 13. I remember my parents' friends looking at a *Vogue* cover of Jerry Hall and saying: 'Look what Mary Greenwell has done!' She opened my eyes to the world of makeup. I became Mary's assistant, attended Glauca Rossi, and the rest is history!

BUILDING THE BRAND

My first job was working with Kate Moss when we were both 19 and kick-starting my career during the incredible supermodel era of the 1980s and '90s, working with all the biggest names. Since then, I've worked with so many iconic actresses, models, and powerhouses – from Kim Kardashian, Cindy Crawford, Penelope Cruz, Salma Hayek, Gigi Hadid and Amal Clooney, to Jennifer Aniston, J K Rowling, Nicole Kidman and Olivia Culpo – the list is endless.

THE INSPIRATION

I have so many female and male role models – they're hugely important. I have a mix of creatives, visionaries and rule breakers that I look to: Helena Rubinstein, Coco Chanel, Walt Disney, Steve Jobs, Winston Churchill, Estée Lauder… You need people who will make you dream and think outside the box! I call upon their energy and help to support me build my empire. I'm constantly learning from what they've achieved, how they thought differently and how they put their own ding in the universe.

I've grown up studying icons (such as Marilyn Monroe, Sofia Loren, Audrey Hepburn and Brigitte Bardot) by really analysing the structure of their faces. All these iconic women are role models for me in the sense that, even though I was only looking at photos, they were teaching me how to make women more beautiful. They were giving me their beauty secrets! And obviously my mother is a great role model for me. She is so full of wisdom and anecdotes: "The sun is beauty suicide" and "Lipstick is instant glamour!"

THE CHALLENGES

People often ask me which challenges I have faced when launching my own brand, and there have been a lot of difficult times over the past three and a half years. However, it really does depend on how you choose to perceive them.

From the very beginning, I've always had a crystal-clear image of how I've wanted my brand to be, and the process of making that vision a reality hasn't always been easy. But I really believe in hard work and pushing yourself, because when you're passionate about something, anything is possible.

Rather than see those experiences as lows, I see them as opportunities and something to learn from. Self-belief is so important – it's just our insecurities that stop us and block us. When someone tells me 'No', I instantly think, "It will be a 'yes'!"

THE LAUNCH

Realising my dreams by launching my own beauty brand was such a pivotal moment in my life. I actually came up with my brand idea at 13, and it developed as I worked as a makeup artist for 25 years. I brought to life through 10 off-the-peg, colour-curated makeup wardrobe looks that embodied the looks I originally created for all my celebrity clients: e.g. the 'Golden Goddess' look for Jennifer Aniston and the 'Rock Chick' look for Kate Moss. It's their incredible beauty DNA that I've extracted and encapsulated into my line. I'm now giving this exclusive red-carpet-ready makeup to everyone!

My vision for my brand has always been incredibly personal, magical and unique. I saw this blank space in the market for makeup that was 'Easy To Use' and 'Easy To Choose' but was also confidence-boosting and woman-to-woman. Women needed the daunting experience of shopping for and wearing makeup de-codified.

I've always wanted to revolutionise and disrupt the beauty industry by launching only the very best products. If a product isn't an innovation or an invention, then I'm not creating it. I won't create any 'me too' products. One of the first hero products that I launched was my miracle-working Magic Cream. I used to mix this backstage to turn around the tired skin of supermodels and celebrities, and they became so obsessed with it that they would ask me for my Magic Cream. It contains Camelia oil, Rosehip oil, Bio-Nymph Peptides and Hyaluronic acid – instantly flooding the skin with moisture. I never apply makeup without it: it gives me the perfect glowing base.

The launch of my #GLOWMO range in 2017 was incredibly exciting – it's guaranteed to make you look and feel your most beautiful and glowing. That summer was all about glow moments, and I wanted to create a range of products that would give you the most gorgeous, natural, enviable glow from dusk till dawn. From the Overnight Bronze and Glow mask that literally gives you the best tan of your life while you sleep and my Beauty Glow palette for the most divine, flattering beauty look to my Unisex Healthy Glow tint moisturiser, I've worked tirelessly to bring women's products to enhance their natural beauty.

SPREADING THE WORD

Social media is so important to getting the word out there. I think the future of sharing beauty expertise and highlighting the latest makeup trends lies predominantly with the increasing rise of social media. It's about strategically using key platforms to Share, Showcase and Simplify makeup looks that will dominate the beauty world over the coming seasons.

Social media will lead the way when it comes to informing and engaging with your consumers, as it allows you to break down key catwalk trends and take them from Runway to Reality. There are so many incredible beauty trends which I've referenced throughout awards season on the red carpet, only to be online literally seconds later. I love that I can do

a look on Emma Roberts for the Oscars and share it instantly on Instagram (which has over 63,000 likes), but then, the day after, live-stream the entire makeover to my fans through Facebook Live!

Social media has given me my own magic media platforms. Facebook has now become one of my main video channels, where I can broadcast live to thousands instantly (with 1.8 billion active monthly users), and Instagram is like having my own glossy publication and billboard (with 600 million active users).

Instagram has a huge impact on my work every day. It's an incredibly powerful tool in engaging your consumer in a deeper relationship than is possible instore, but also for expressing your brand DNA. It gives instant access to behind-the-scenes content and sharing artistry and expertise. It also gives me instant access to street-style beauty trends that I wouldn't normally see (such as the unicorn trend) and allows me to ask about and understand much better my consumer needs. By reading comments under posts, I can work out which looks they love and the type of expert tricks they want to learn. I also love engaging my Instagram community in naming lipstick shades and making key suggestions for the brand!

CHARLOTTE'S TIPS

- *I think success is about having a single-minded focus, visualising success, dreaming big, daring to make that dream a reality and self-belief.*

- *Life is limitless!*

- *Always reach for the stars. I always talk about the power of visualisation. Visualise what you want, and don't give up until you get it!*

> *THERE ARE STILL MANY CAUSES WORTH SACRIFICING FOR, SO MUCH HISTORY YET TO BE MADE.*
>
> **MICHELLE OBAMA**

ELLE MACPHERSON

BUSINESSWOMAN, SUPERMODEL, MOTHER, CO-FOUNDER OF WELLECO

Elle Macpherson is an Australian model, businesswoman and TV presenter. She is the founder and co-owner of her lingerie brand, Elle Macpherson Body. In 2014, she co-founded WelleCo and released its flagship product, The Super Elixir.

I realised early on in my career that it would be best if I could create content and produce my own independent material. I left traditional model agencies to form my own company, Elle Macpherson Inc, when I was 25 years old. I partnered with a fantastic business manager who helped teach me to be the creator of my career. From there, I licensed my name in various categories, built a strong 30-year lingerie business, produced swimsuit calendars and created content for network TV. I started to produce and host various TV shows (as the executive producer), including *Fashion Star* for NBC and Top Model UK. Today, my business strategies have evolved, and I am a passionate co-founder and co-owner of wellness company WelleCo. I co-own a 50/50 joint venture with Elle Macpherson Body.

THE EVOLUTION OF THE SUPER ELIXIR
I discovered the profound benefit of good nutrition and living Alkaline from my Nutritional Doctor, Dr Simone Laubscher, and I wanted to share it. The most important thing to me is how I feel and I've found if my body is getting the nutrients it needs, then it shows on the outside – beauty from the inside out.

I teamed up with Andrea Bux (another Aussie and founder of Invisible Zinc) to form WelleCo. We knew there would be easier products to start with, but our Super Elixir Alkalising Greens are the core of WelleCo, and why we exist, so we began with that. We tested the product for years, changing and modifying it to develop the perfect formula. Yes, it took time to communicate properly, but our customers started doing the talking for us. The more people who discovered and started taking the Super Elixir, the more they wanted to share it. It grew organically, you could say.

It's been a fast trajectory upwards ever since, with a huge growth in staff and wellness products that we now offer: Nourishing Protein, Sleep Welle Calming Tea, Kids Protein and a wonderful Alkalising Greens gold caddy collaboration with Aerin Lauder.

I attribute its success to it being a great, quality product and an honest story.

It's easily accessible, delivered to your doorstep, and it works!

CAREER LONGEVITY

Love, laughter and water! I believe in courage, co-operation, perseverance, passion and being the creator of your own life – I've found if you do what you love and love what you do, the by-product is success!

DAILY ROUTINE

I used to have a strict routine that I followed of high intensity training, but now I am about listening to my body and mixing it up. When I wake up I think about what it is my body really needs, it might be a swim in the ocean or walk along the beach, yoga with friends or a boxing class. I believe mixing things up is fun and helps with motivation so each day is different.

WELLECO – A PIONEER IN THE BEAUTY ARENA

I am proud over the past few years WelleCo has been spearheading one of the biggest shifts in beauty with ingestible challenging traditional customer behaviour.

Beauty from the inside was so compelling to me that I dedicated our business to it. The future of beauty is from the inside, and the future of ingestible is going to be natural, absorbable and food based. I believe you should care about your health and how you feel first, the rest will come.

ELLE'S TIPS

- *Find co-dreamers: people who understand and support your dreams.*

- *Visualise exactly what you want to create in detail.*

- *Write, collect images and make mood boards.*

- *Share dreams and watch them grow.*

- *Appreciate all the baby steps it takes to make a leap forward.*

- *Jump, and the net will appear.*

KAREN GEE

ENTREPRENEUR AND FASHION DESIGNER

Karen Gee is the Founder of global luxury fashion brand, Karen Gee.

I was born in Rockhampton, Queensland, Australia, and from a young age, my life revolved around working in our family businesses. These included the local skating rink, a plant shop, an ice cream shop, a photo shop, and council swimming pools. Unlike many of my peers, my childhood wasn't filled with leisurely weekends or social outings – I spent my mornings, evenings, and most weekends working. However one of the joys was that some of my school friends were actually employed at these businesses as juniors to earn their pocket money!

At the time, I often felt like I was missing out, watching my friends enjoy their freedom while I was expected to contribute. But in hindsight, those years gifted me some of life's most valuable lessons – the true meaning of hard work, the ability to connect with people, and the importance of resilience. I learned how to communicate, network, and build meaningful relationships, both personally and professionally.

I was quite a sporty girl, loving netball and playing squash, and for many years I took part in ballet lessons, however, I was never the prima ballerina, with two left feet, and never naturally gifted when it came to dance, but it allowed me to be with my friends and have a good laugh and wear beautiful costumes! I never took myself too seriously.

Life wasn't always easy; we experienced extraordinary challenges, but we also had incredible moments of joy. That contrast has given me a deep appreciation for life's highs and lows. Looking back, I wouldn't change a thing – I am forever grateful for the foundation my parents gave me through their unwavering dedication and work ethic.

LAUNCHING KAREN GEE

My story isn't the traditional one of attending fashion school, working for established labels, and then launching my own brand. Instead, it unfolded in a way I could never have predicted.

Whilst raising five children and dedicating myself to being the best mother I could be, I developed a deep fear of losing my own identity. I understood that children grow up, build their own lives, and become less dependent on their parents. I didn't want to wake up one day and feel as though I had nothing that was truly mine – nothing I had built through my own hard work and ambition.

MRS AUSTRALIA

Unexpectedly, one of my sons (unannounced to me) entered me into the Mrs Australia pageant, where I became a state finalist and ultimately won the title of Mrs Australia 2011. It was a huge honour, but I never saw it as a title to simply wear – I saw it as an opportunity to make a difference.

Throughout my reign, I became a global ambassador for brands such as Hilton Hotel, Lorna Jane, and Australian Racing, and I worked closely with the Butterfly Foundation, which supports individuals with eating disorders and body dissatisfaction.

After my year of service, I wanted to take everything I had learned and create something meaningful.

I wanted to blend my love for fashion, luxury design, and empowering women – regardless of their shape or size – into something unique. And so, in 2012, Karen Gee was born.

I had no formal training, no industry connections, and no experience in design. I didn't even know how to construct a dress. But I had determination, and Google became my best friend. I spent countless hours teaching myself everything I needed to know, working day and night to bring my vision to life.

By 2015, demand for my designs had grown so much that I opened my flagship store in the heart of Sydney. I also invested in a full-scale production house in Australia, building out a team of patternmakers, machinists, and a production and marketing team.

My journey into fashion wasn't conventional, but it was built on passion, perseverance, and a deep desire to create something that empowers women.

CHALLENGES

There have been many moments in my journey where I've felt a deep sense of defeat. One of the most challenging times was in the early days of building my brand. I had no formal training in fashion, no industry connections, and no idea how to navigate this new world I had stepped into.

There were days when I felt completely out of my depth – the whole imposter syndrome as well as production challenges, and the fear that I had taken on something way beyond me. In the early days, I faced a lot of setbacks that made me question whether I had made the right decision. I remember feeling exhausted, overwhelmed, and doubting whether I could keep going. Countless times I considered giving it all away. But what got me through was my mindset, and the support of the ones closest to me. I reminded myself why I started: to create something meaningful, to empower women, and to build something I could be proud of. Instead of letting challenges define me, I used it as a lesson. I leaned on my resilience, sought advice from people I trusted, and broke things down into smaller, manageable steps.

CAREER TURNING POINT

There have been several defining moments for Karen Gee, but one of the biggest turning points was when the Duchess of Sussex, Meghan Markle, wore one of my dresses during her first official visit to Australia in 2018. Overnight, my brand gained international recognition, and the demand skyrocketed. Orders flooded in from all over the world, (the website struggled) and the exposure placed Karen Gee on a global stage. It was a surreal moment – one that reinforced my belief in what I had built and the power of timeless, elegant design.

Beyond that, another significant turning point was the realisation that my brand was not just about fashion – it was about empowering women and as the brand grew, we knew that our vision and passion was infectious. The ethos behind Karen Gee has always been to make women feel confident, beautiful, and strong, no matter their shape or size. Seeing how my designs transformed the way women carried themselves was a powerful shift. It became clear that I wasn't just selling dresses; I was creating pieces that gave women a sense of confidence and self-assurance.

Another key moment was the decision to keep my production process for Made to Measure in Australia.

At a time when many brands were outsourcing, I chose to invest in local craftsmanship, ensuring that every piece was made with the highest quality and care. This decision solidified my commitment to ethical production and maintaining a personal connection to every aspect of my brand.

Each of these moments shaped the trajectory of Karen Gee, reinforcing the values of quality, empowerment, and timeless design.

CAREER SUCCESS

The success of Karen Gee has always been rooted in timeless design, impeccable craftsmanship, and a deep commitment to empowering women. While having royalty and celebrities wear my brand has been an incredible honour, I have the deepest appreciation for those who are consistently loyal to the brand and our values, my long-term vision extends far beyond high-profile recognition. My goal is to expand Karen Gee into a truly global luxury brand while staying true to my core values – quality and inclusivity.

Building strong relationships, surrounding yourself with the right team, and staying true to your values will always be more important than any trend or moment of recognition. Assembling the right team was one of the biggest challenges – not just in terms of skill but in finding individuals who share the same passion and values. I'm incredibly grateful to be surrounded by a team that believes in our vision and brings it to life every day.

BUILDING A BRAND

What makes us unique is our commitment to creating elegant designs that celebrate every woman, regardless of shape or size. We believe true style is universal, and every woman deserves to feel confident and powerful in what she wears. Our made to measure service goes beyond just a perfect fit – it's a deeply personal experience where we listen, understand, and tailor each piece to complement the individual.

Karen Gee is more than just a label; it's a statement of individuality and empowerment. I built the brand based on principles that matter – quality, timeless design, and the belief that every woman deserves to feel confident and unique. In a landscape that often values conformity, I chose to celebrate authenticity, and that's what sets Karen Gee apart.

DEFINING MOMENT OF SUCCESS

A defining moment for me wasn't a single public event, but rather a quiet, personal realisation that transformed my vision for Karen Gee.

One day, I received a heartfelt note from a customer who shared how one of my designs had given her the confidence to overcome a difficult period in her life. In that moment, I understood that my work wasn't just about creating beautiful garments – it was about empowering women and making a tangible difference in their lives. This experience reaffirmed that every challenge I'd faced and every lesson I'd learned was worth it, because it enabled me to craft pieces that resonate deeply with women. It was a powerful reminder that true success lies in the impact we have on others, and it has since fueled my commitment to designing with purpose and passion.

LESSONS LEARNED

I am learning every single day, and I truly hope I will continue to learn for a very long time.

One of the biggest lessons has been that there is no perfect road map to success. When I started Karen Gee, I had no formal training in fashion, no industry connections

– just a vision and a willingness to work hard. I've learned that sometimes, the best way forward is simply to take the first step, even if you don't have all the answers.

ADVICE FOR SUCCESS

Success looks different to everyone. For some, it's measured by wealth; for others, it's about popularity or demand. But for me, success is doing something you love and having people love what you do.

At the end of the day, success isn't just about reaching a destination – it's about enjoying the journey, staying true to yourself, and making an impact in a way that's meaningful to you.

I've also learned the importance of resilience. There have been moments of doubt, setbacks, and challenges that felt overwhelming, however I now understand that failure is not the opposite of success – it's part of it. Every challenge has taught me something valuable and ultimately made my brand stronger.

Another lesson that stands out is the power of listening.

The women who wear Karen Gee have shaped the brand more than anything else. Their feedback, their confidence, and their trust in my designs have guided so many decisions along the way.

It's about the people. Building strong relationships, surrounding yourself with the right team, and staying true to your values will always be more important than any trend or moment of recognition.

Each day is a new opportunity to grow, and I welcome that with open arms. Stay true to yourself, trust your instincts, and success will follow.

In a world that can sometimes feel cut throat, I've always chosen to lift others up rather than tear them down – I simply don't understand the mentality of competition at the expense of kindness.

QUALITIES FOR SUCCESS

First and foremost, hard work. Nothing truly meaningful comes without effort. Being willing to put in the time, even when no one is watching, is what separates those who dream from those who achieve.

Then there's resilience. Life is full of setbacks, and no journey is without its challenges. The ability to pick yourself up, learn from mistakes, and keep going is what keeps dreams alive.

Humility is just as important. Success should never make someone feel above others. Staying grounded, learning from those around you, and remembering where you started keeps success meaningful.

Lastly, kindness and integrity. Treating people well, doing the right thing, and lifting others up along the way is, to me, the greatest form of success. If you can go to bed each night knowing you've worked hard, been true to yourself, made a positive impact – then feel grateful you're already successful.

INSPIRATION

My mum has always been a constant in my life. Watching her navigate business and life with such calmness and grace, even in the most stressful situations, has shaped so much of who I am. She's shown me the power of resilience and kindness, and that true strength often comes from the way you carry yourself, no matter what's going on around you.

The foundation of my success and happiness lies in the love and support of my family. My husband and five children have been my backbone on this incredible journey. They are my world, and my greatest achievement in life is the family I've been blessed to nurture and share this journey with. Every day, I feel deeply grateful to have six amazing souls by my side who support, love, and never judge me. They cheer me on, sharing in both my triumphs and my struggles, and always reminding me of what truly matters. Their unwavering belief in me allows me to keep pushing forward, to chase my dreams, and to approach life with a spirit of resilience and purpose. I am entirely grateful that I get to share my life with such incredible people. Their love is my strength, and our bond is the greatest gift.

KAREN'S ADVICE

- *Passion & Purpose* – You need to truly love what you do. Passion fuels perseverance, and when you have a deep connection to your work, challenges become opportunities rather than obstacles.

- *Resilience* – The path to success is never linear. There will be setbacks, failures, and moments of doubt, but resilience and continuous learning is what keeps you going when things get tough.

- *Hard Work & Dedication* – There's no substitute for hard work. Success doesn't happen overnight, it's built through consistent effort, discipline, and an unwavering commitment to your goals.

- *Integrity & Authenticity* – Staying true to yourself and your values is crucial. People connect with authenticity and success that is built on honesty, respect and purpose will always be more fulfilling.

- *A Strong Support Network* – No one achieves success alone. Surrounding yourself with people who uplift, challenge and inspire you.

OLIVIA PALERMO

ENTREPRENEUR

Olivia Palermo is an international fashion and beauty icon who found fame after being cast in the reality television series The City, *which followed the professional lives of young women based in New York City. She has since graced the covers of dozens of magazines across the globe and has cemented herself as a true style icon of her generation.*

Even at a young age, I was passionate about fashion and naturally sought to grow within an industry that I loved. I began by studying at the American University in Paris, where I was fortunate enough to receive my first professional experience, as an intern at *Quest magazine*. It was there that I gained insight into how a magazine should run, along with learning first-hand about all the different facets within the industry.

At Quest, I had the opportunity to work with the magazine's market editor, which involved discovering new designers, meeting with interior decorators, and finding interesting venues for various projects. It was a wonderful way for me to get exposure within the fashion and editorial worlds, enabling me with a strong foundation for future positions, like at *Elle* magazine, and helping me gain foresight into what possible directions I wanted to take my career next.

THE CITY

Initially, Viacom contacted my former agent to inquire whether I would be interested in participating in the reality television show *The City*. The show was not what I expected because of scripting; however, the decision to participate in the show was not difficult, and I might not be where I am today if I had turned down the opportunity. The show's exposure allowed me to be heard and recognised on a global scale, which was a unique opportunity for me at that time.

I received an intern role at Diane von Furstenberg as part of filming the show. I look up to so many women in and out of the industry, but I have always held Diane von Furstenberg in high regard. I feel as though she is a pioneer for a certain type of woman in the market and has done so much for emerging talent, so it was great to get to work with her.

After the show, I focused full-time on Wilhelmina International, a talent and model management agency, to build my brand.

BUILDING THE OLIVIA PALERMO BRAND

The motivation behind my website, oliviapalermo.com, was to document travel locations that I enjoyed as well as to build a platform using my own voice for style. Subsequently, it has evolved into a lifestyle and editorial website reflecting my aesthetic, while supporting emerging young designers. Each year, on average, the website attracts an audience of passionate supporters from over 220 countries.

I currently work with many different brands, including campaigns for AERIN and MAX&Co, and on a larger scale as Global Brand Ambassador for Banana Republic. In addition to my ambassadorship role, I have co-designed a capsule collection with Banana Republic, launching in the autumn of 2017. We're a great team, and it's been a collaborative approach that reflects the synergy between my style and the Banana Republic brand. Overall, I believe my brand represents an ever-evolving, fresh perspective on contemporary classics that is relatable to women of all ages.

GETTING SOCIAL

My view of social media has evolved, and I have learned from experience and continue to do so. Whereas before it would be an outfit post or a piece of jewellery that I liked, it is now such a useful tool to share what I think about fashion, beauty and culture. It's great to be able to communicate with designers and users in a new way. I can express myself and my style – whether it be a picture on Instagram, sharing a story on my website or providing inspiration for an upcoming shoot on Pinterest. I think it's fascinating how direct and powerful these social media platforms have become for myself and my brand.

THE CHALLENGES

I face challenges head-on every day, which helps me learn more and allows me to continue evolving. I feel that a big contributor to my success has been surrounding myself with a smart, tight-knit team, as they are a reflection of myself and my brand. This has enabled me to build and grow a brand that is organic and true to my vision. As for the future of my brand? You will have to wait and see!

OLIVIA'S TIPS

- *Try different roles within an industry in order to decide the path you would like to pursue.*

- *Let your hard work speak for itself.*

- *Always be pulled together, as it sets your mind to be productive.*

ABEER STOUHI

FOUNDER OF GLAMODA

Abeer Stouhi, the founder and creative mind behind the Lebanese ready-to-wear label Glamoda, embarked on her fashion journey half a decade ago. Abeer blends contemporary trends with a vintage flair and has a passion for crafting chic women's suits.

Looking back at my younger years, my interests may seem somewhat eclectic at first glance. While many of my peers were diving into typical hobbies and activities, I found myself drawn to a different path altogether. You see, even from a young age, I had a deep-rooted passion for social justice and advocacy. It was a calling that led me to pursue a degree in social work at university and ultimately dedicate nearly a decade of my life to working on behalf of marginalised communities, particularly women and children.

But amidst my commitment to social activism, there was another passion quietly simmering beneath the surface: fashion. Specifically, I was enamoured with the timeless allure of vintage suits and the iconic styles of fashion legends like Grace Kelly, Audrey Hepburn and Sophia Loren.

It may seem like an unlikely pairing – social work and fashion – but for me, they were two sides of the same coin. Both allowed me to express myself creatively and make a positive impact on the world around me, albeit in different ways.

My interest in fashion wasn't just about aesthetics; it was about empowerment and self-expression. I believe that what we wear can be a powerful form of communication, reflecting our personality, values, and aspirations.

And so, armed with this dual passion for social justice and fashion, I embarked on a journey to merge the two worlds. In 2018, I founded Glamoda with a simple yet ambitious mission: to offer stylish, modern suits that didn't compromise on youthfulness. Since then, Glamoda has grown beyond my wildest dreams, becoming a dominant force in Lebanon's fashion scene and earning recognition across the Arab region. And while my interests may have evolved over the years, my commitment to empowering others and fostering self-expression remains unwavering.

So, when people ask me about my interests when I was young, I tell them about my love for social justice, my fascination with fashion, and the journey that led me to where I am today. It's a story of passion, purpose and the power of pursuing your dreams, no matter where they may lead.

BUILDING MY CAREER
My journey into the fashion industry started a bit later in life. In my youth, I was deeply passionate about social work and dedicated nearly a decade to advocating for the rights of children and women. Even today, I continue this fight as a member of the committee of one of Lebanon's most influential NGOs.

Reflecting on my transition from social work to fashion, I recall a vivid memory from my university days. During my university years, I would attend classes dressed in suits, and my admiration for classic style was evident to all. However, it was during a practice session in one of Beirut's most impoverished and neglected areas, known as the "Red Zone," that a pivotal moment occurred. My trainer, seeking to impart a lesson about the importance of dressing appropriately for social work, placed me in this challenging environment. I remember her words vividly: "This is a lesson for you to understand how you should present yourself from now on."

This experience served as a catalyst for me to pursue my passion for fashion more earnestly. It was a realisation that while my heart remained dedicated to social causes, my soul also craved the creativity and self-expression found in the world of fashion. This intersection of compassion and style ultimately propelled me to embark on a new journey, one where I could merge my love for advocacy with my fascination for design and aesthetics.

Today, as the founder of Glamoda, I am proud to channel my diverse experiences and passions into a platform that celebrates individuality and empowerment through fashion. My journey from social work to fashion exemplifies the transformative power of following one's heart and embracing new opportunities, no matter where life may lead.

STARTING GLAMODA
Well, my journey into the world of fashion wasn't exactly a straight path. While I was fascinated with suits – their elegance and their sophistication – every time I tried to find one that suited my style, I ended up feeling like it aged me beyond my years.

It was a frustrating realisation, especially since I couldn't find modern, stylish options that captured the essence of youthfulness. That's when the idea struck me – why not create what I couldn't find? And just like that, Glamoda was born in 2018.

Over the next five years, we made waves in the ready-to-wear market in Lebanon, carving out a niche for ourselves with our unique blend of vintage charm and contemporary flair. It was incredibly rewarding to see our vision resonating with people, not just locally but across the Arab region.

Then came 2024, a milestone year for us. We took a bold step onto the international stage, showcasing Glamoda's creations at the prestigious Paris Fashion Week. The experience was nothing short of surreal – being surrounded by industry giants and sharing our designs with a global audience.

The response was overwhelmingly positive, and it was heartening to hear people praising the beauty, elegance and uniqueness of our designs. What struck a chord with many was our ability to seamlessly merge classic elements with modern trends – something that has always been at the core of Glamoda's identity. For me, that moment in Paris was more than just a showcase of our work; it was a validation of our journey and a testament to the endless possibilities that come with pursuing your passion. And as we continue to grow and evolve, I'm excited to see where this journey takes us next.

On August 4, 2020, I was a victim of the Beirut blast, the third biggest explosion in the world.

I suffered severe injuries, leaving me terrified and unable to move. I underwent numerous critical surgeries for my face, which was shattered, and I had multiple broken bones throughout my body. My house, Glamoda's showroom and its workshop were all destroyed as well.

Back in that hospital bed, feeling utterly broken, it was the fragments of hope that kept me going. I clung to every shred of faith and chose strength for my children and family. They needed me to rise above this, not for myself, but for them. It was not a time for grief but for resilience. That night, I felt a surge of power. I knew I had to fight for my dreams, for my family, and for all the resilient people of Lebanon. I had to show the world that we were not broken, that we were unstoppable!

Even in the midst of this unimaginable chaos, with a body weakened by injuries, my spirit remained resolute. During this very difficult time, Glamoda's first international campaign was launched, and it achieved remarkable success.

QUALITIES FOR SUCCESS
Success thrives on a potent blend of vision, creativity and self-belief. If you are creative and have passion for what you do, you need to focus, make a plan to reach your goals, and work on improving your skills to transform your vision into reality. Never stop working hard! It's also so important not to be distracted by people who try to destroy your confidence.

I don't think that I was inspired by only one person, or at least a specific one! I was always fascinated by each and every elegant and confident woman, even if she was not famous. I love the aura they leave around them when they enter a place. That is what I try to translate into my designs and into Glamoda's essence: a woman distinguished by her timeless elegance and confidence.

FUTURE
Like every designer, I dream of Glamoda's global expansion, particularly into European markets. Through franchising and strategic initiatives, Glamoda aspires to become a prominent presence in the global fashion landscape, embodying elegance, confidence, and timeless style.

ABEER'S ADVICE

- *Embrace your uniqueness and hold fast to your vision.*

- *Shun distractions, focus on personal growth, and strive to outdo yourself, not others.*

- *Maintain integrity, persevere, and work hard, knowing that success blossoms from dedication and passion.*

CONSISTENTLY ASK YOURSELF, WHAT COULD GO WRONG? ARE WE INNOVATING ENOUGH?, ARE WE MANAGING EFFECTIVELY? THIS MINDSET OF VIGILANCE, INNOVATION, AND CONTINUOUS IMPROVEMENT IS ESSENTIAL FOR BUILDING AND SUSTAINING A SUCCESSFUL BUSINESS.

BERNARD ARNAULT (CEO, LVMH)

LEANNE ROBERS

CO-FOUNDER OF SHE LOVES TECH

Leanne Robers is Co-Founder of She Loves Tech, the world's largest startup competition and accelerator programme for women-led and women-impact tech startups. Now operating in 76 countries, She Loves Tech is committed to building an ecosystem for technology, entrepreneurship and innovation that creates opportunities for women and closes the gender gap in startup funding.

Both my parents have the biggest hearts. Even though my paternal grandparents wanted my dad to study business or be a doctor, he wanted to be a missionary. He later studied Psychology and completed his PhD, working as a janitor in a school to support himself through his studies in the US and to provide for me (who was seven months old when we moved to the US). After his post-doctorate, we moved back to Singapore, where he was one of the first psychologists in Singapore to open a private clinical psychology clinic. This was a time when going to a psychologist was still highly stigmatised. He knew his mission was to help others, and he persevered as he knew it was the right thing to do and people needed good psychological services to help them overcome their personal struggles. Having a unique surname, "Robers", and living in a country in Asia, I constantly have people coming up to me asking me if I'm related to Dr Harold Robers. When I would very excitedly tell them that he's my father, they would proceed to tell me their stories – "Your dad saved my life", "Your dad saved my marriage", "Your dad helped me along so much in my career", "Your dad helped my children greatly and now they are doing so well". My dad was never focused on building wealth – he set his eye on doing good. And that's what I aimed to do in my life – to ensure that whatever I did, it was about the impact that I created.

CAREER BEGINNING

I was a Psychology major at university – I didn't have any technical or computer science training. I was fortunate to land a job at Siemens UK. While going through the management trainee programme, my employer needed someone to create an internal SharePoint site. I volunteered to do it because I wanted to challenge myself and develop a new skill, even though I was not an obvious choice. I needed to learn HTML and CSS, and I did all the things you'd expect – read books and articles and ask friends for advice – but the most important thing I did was to learn by doing and not to be paralysed by uncertainty or by the fear of failing. I allowed myself to try and even be bad at it sometimes and ask for help when I was stuck. This experience started me on a path to becoming a leader in tech. It gave me some practical skills and a basic understanding of programming that have proven extremely useful as an entrepreneur working with engineers. Second, it showed me I didn't have to be afraid of tech because I proved I could try, make mistakes and learn. After the programme, I was hired into another division in Siemens – Siemens Automation, dealing with rail infrastructure and railway systems. Out of 200 applicants, I came up as the top candidate but also the youngest. I found myself, a young female Asian, managing project teams of white male engineers with ten to twenty years more experience. On top of the job's inherent challenges, it was clear that these teams did not want to be led by a young woman. I was even told many times to wear glasses and a wedding ring just to look older, and to learn how to play golf to fit in with the boys. During this time, I battled immensely with identity. I was constantly worried about how I could provide strong and capable leadership without the risks of being seen as trying too hard to be like the men or exploiting my femininity. My experience led me to realise that while welfare in the workplace has greatly improved, the mantle of leadership nevertheless requires a woman to make very careful, deliberate choices at work. Instead of running away or conforming to gender stereotypes, I decided to step up to resolve the issues I faced. I had a fantastic manager, and he helped me isolate areas of inadequacy and worked with me to build up my technical knowledge before I spoke with senior engineers. Importantly, he reminded me to bring fresh perspectives to each meeting, and I gradually gained confidence and became more assertive in my interactions. I learnt to actively find ways to leverage the unique strengths and qualities that I could bring to the table. I also quickly learnt that leadership requires authenticity and self-confidence to avoid being caught up by the desire to be liked and respected. My relationship with teams improved, and this allowed me to focus on leading my team through successful projects and bids.

STARTING 'SHE LOVES TECH'

After Siemens, I embarked on a new journey as a tech entrepreneur, founding three companies in diverse domains: real estate and hospitality, Fintech, and art and technology. Being a tech entrepreneur is hard, but being a woman tech entrepreneur is even harder. Pervasive biases, a scarcity of resources tailored for women, and a lack of female role models often lead to isolation and loneliness. During this period, I met Virginia Tan. She was running Lean In China, a community for women professionals in China, and she had launched, with Rhea See, a startup competition for women called She Loves Tech. As a founder who had been through the challenges of navigating a male-dominated industry and investor landscape, I saw the potential that a platform like She Loves Tech could have to showcase and support women tech entrepreneurs. I loved their mission. I was inspired by the potential of what She Loves Tech could grow into. I joined Virginia and Rhea as cofounder, and now we're the world's largest organisation dedicated to taking women entrepreneurs to the next level.

CREATING OPPORTUNITIES FOR WOMEN

She Loves Tech is a global platform for entrepreneurship, technology and innovation for women-led and women-impact startups. She Loves Tech originated in 2015 as a startup competition, helping women-led or women-impact businesses to receive more investments, and has grown into the world's largest startup competition and accelerator programme for women and technology, having worked with over 15,000 startups from 107 countries. Together with its education and acceleration programs, She Loves Tech has been working to close the funding gap for women. To date, startup finalists from the She Loves Tech competition programme have successfully raised close to 600M USD in funding. She Loves Tech has a large network of investors, mentors, experts, local partners in the startup space and more than 700 partners (corporates, venture capital funds and other accelerators/incubators) in our community. Through our experience working with women entrepreneurs over the last nine years, we understand the nuanced challenges that women tech founders face and provide them with the tools, resources, networks and access to capital to help them grow and scale.

TURNING POINT

Understanding that while failure by itself is not a good thing, failure, where you *learn* from it, can be a really good thing. So, for me, I re-framed "failure" to become "running a series of experiments". When something doesn't work, you adjust your hypothesis and run the experiment again.

CHALLENGES

As a young girl, I always thought that having the "perfect life" was what I wanted – finding my Prince Charming, building the perfect family, having the perfect job and living happily ever after. However, I felt so much pressure to live this life that I really struggled and fell into depression when I couldn't meet this unrealistic expectation. During that time, I was really hard on myself and I felt like I wasn't doing enough and that I wasn't capable enough, wasn't smart enough, wasn't pretty enough. I was my harshest critic, and it wasn't productive. One day, someone asked me, "Leanne, until you learn to respect yourself, how do you expect others to respect you?" That wasn't easy to hear, but it was necessary for me at that moment. It was a hard journey to love and respect myself. And I don't think I'm 100% there yet. But what I learnt was that every experience, especially the things that didn't work out, was getting closer to my ideal self. Every moment, good and bad, is part of my growth, and all are achievements in their own right. I also found the "perfect" husband, one whose quiet confidence blew me away and who is my biggest cheerleader. He always believes in me, even when I don't believe in myself. He taught me that to love him fully, I needed to first love myself.

I would like to be remembered as someone who significantly contributed to closing the gender gap in technology and entrepreneurship. I've aimed to empower them by providing them with the platform, resources, and network they need to thrive. It's about creating a global impact by influencing the ecosystem to support women in technology.

LEANNE'S TIPS

- *Confidently advocate for yourself. It's important to talk about your accomplishments to help other people understand your value.*

- *Network – keep building a diverse network. The best time to build a network is when you don't need it and ensure you form relationships that are built on trust.*

- *Tech is a means to an end, not an end in itself. Make sure you're solving an important problem and let the tech follow the problem, not the other way around.*

- *Self-care is not an indulgence; it's essential for our productivity.*

- *Be kind to ourselves and allow ourselves to focus on what truly matters.*

BRIA FLEMING

FASHION DESIGNER, REALITY TV STAR, FASHION ICON

STARTING IN THE FASHION INDUSTRY
When I was a little girl, I was obsessed with watching *America's Next Top Model*. I loved the glamorous side of the show as well as the unique clothing they styled the women in. From there, I started creating my crop tops and selling them at school and online. Fast-forward to now, and I was able to save up funds to invest in a bigger clothing line.

ADVICE TO WOMEN
Be confident, authentic, and persistent. Embrace your unique style and vision while staying open to learning and adapting to trends. Network and build connections, as the fashion industry often relies heavily on relationships.

FIRST BIG BREAK
My first break into the industry was back in 2012. I was designing custom tank-tops and selling them at school and online.

CHALLENGES
The fashion industry can be highly competitive and demanding. Some of the biggest challenges I faced included breaking into the market, and dealing with fast-changing trends, production issues and financial constraints. Staying resilient and adaptable, and continuously learning are essential traits for overcoming these challenges.

ADVICE FOR SUCCESS
Focus on developing your own creative voice and signature style. Be innovative, think outside the box and stay true to your vision. Embrace sustainability and ethical practices, as consumers increasingly value these aspects.

In the fashion industry, failures are common but can be valuable learning experiences. Many successful individuals have faced setbacks and failures before achieving recognition. Success often comes with perseverance, a willingness to learn from mistakes, adaptability to changing market demands and staying true to one's vision and style. It's essential to celebrate successes, learn from failures, and continuously improve to thrive in the dynamic world of fashion. Remember, the fashion industry is constantly evolving, and success often requires a combination of talent, hard work, and an innovative mindset.

YOUR PASSION FOR STYLE
I'm inspired by culture, art, music, historical eras and personal experiences.

POWER OF SOCIAL MEDIA
Social media has become a powerful tool for the fashion industry. It allows designers, brands and influencers to reach a broader audience, showcase their work and connect with potential customers. Utilising social media strategically can significantly impact a career in fashion.

LEONIE HANNE

FASHION INFLUENCER

Leonie Hanne is a world-renowned fashion influencer.

STARTING IN THE FASHION INDUSTRY
I was studying and working before I gained a management degree in Business and then went on to work at Germany's biggest fashion online retailer, the Otto Group, whilst also studying textile and fashion management at night. This dual system was hard but rewarding, I loved what I did and had a steady career laid out.

Initially, I signed up to Instagram and started my blog as a way to showcase my love of fashion; it was a creative and personal outlet for me. At the time, I didn't know that Instagram would become such a huge part of my business, as it was such a new concept and there were no previous success stories I could look up to.

When I attended my first fashion week, my Instagram account only had 1,000 followers, but I started generating sales quite quickly. Soon after, Tory Burch became the first large international brand I worked with, as they invited me to New York Fashion Week. Today I'm lucky to work with my dream brands such as Gucci, Prada, and Valentino. For Valentino, I've been working on amazing editorial shoots such as *Vogue* Turkey and a *Harper's Bazaar Brasil* cover story I'm very proud of.

ADVICE ON WORKING IN THE INDUSTRY
The digital fashion industry didn't exist in the same way as it does now. There was nobody to give me advice, and there were no examples to follow. It was all very unknown, so I just had to trust myself and my instincts. You can open so many doors for yourself if you're hardworking, resilient and you believe in your own abilities. Focus on your self-belief, and you can achieve anything you set your mind to.

WORKING AS A STYLE INFLUENCER
My main aim is to encourage women across the world to explore their unique sense of style and pursue their passions. Female empowerment is very important to me, particularly given my experiences in a corporate career and the fashion industry, as I know how hard and competitive these industries are. I mainly want to inspire people by setting an example and educating them on how they can elevate their own wardrobes and self-confidence by using fashion as a form of self-expression.

YOUR PASSION FOR WORKING AS AN INFLUENCER
I love working as a model, but at the moment my content creation work takes up a lot of time. As a teenager I would always buy copies of my favourite magazines such as *InStyle Germany*. I just always loved the fashion editorials and never could have predicted that my dream of being featured in one would come true. Let alone a cover! It's definitely something I'd like to pursue more in the future.

YOUR BIGGEST CHALLENGE
Developing my confidence has always been my biggest challenge! When I first started, I was so shy, I could barely look into a camera. The more confident I got with my work and the more comfortable I got in front of the camera, the more I

understood the direction I wanted to go in. The more I started establishing relationships with brands, the more self-assured I felt.

THE MISCONCEPTION OF FASHION INFLUENCERS HAVING A GLAMOROUS LIFE
I think the most common misconception is that influencers come from a money background or have any similar kind of advantages to make a career in fashion, but every creator is different. I always worked and studied hard. I don't come from money, but I have a good fashion sense, so people don't always see the dedication and amount of strategic work that goes into everything. The reality is that all of the big bloggers I know are so inspiring; they're talented businesswomen. But because the fashion and beauty industries can be perceived as superficial in comparison to others, many people forget the entrepreneurial, creative side of things.

LEONIE'S TIPS

- *You can open so many doors for yourself if you're hardworking and resilient and you believe in your own abilities.*

- *Focus on your self-belief, and you can achieve anything you set your mind to.*

NEVER DOUBT THAT YOU ARE VALUABLE AND POWERFUL AND DESERVING OF EVERY CHANCE IN THE WORLD TO PURSUE YOUR DREAMS.

HILLARY CLINTON

PARIS HILINSKI

FASHION ICON, GOLFING PRO

Golfing pro legend Paris Hilinski is a worldwide icon after first tagging Virgil Abloh on social media. She has collaborated with Oakley, Louis Vuitton and more.

BREAKING INTO THE FASHION INDUSTRY
I started playing golf when I was just about 14 years old. A year later, I qualified for the US Open and was thrown into the world of professional golf. After spending a few years playing, I realised there was little voice for women in the sport to decide and have a say over what they wear and compete in. At 17, I decided I wanted to try something different, so I screwed cleats into a pair of Off-White label sneakers. After playing well in them, I posted it to social media and sent a note to the late Virgil Abloh, Off-White's founder. He responded the very next day, and we built a relationship via phone calls, texts, and social media that consisted of long, inspirational discussions on our ideas and passions. He understood and wholeheartedly believed in my goals. He gave me my push into the fashion industry, and it's given me the power to grow my sport and empower other women within the industry.

CHALLENGES
As a young woman in a male-dominated industry, I've learned to overcome challenges that attempt to underestimate my ability in not only my sport but business as well. I've learned to focus on my bigger goals and channel all my energy into helping bring culture and diversity into the sport of golf and continue Virgil's passion for doing the same within the fashion industry.

ADVICE FOR WOMEN
To be bold and dream big is a great thing. As a woman, you often get told no and are expected to sit back and listen. Never take no for an answer and never be afraid to ask for more. The best piece of advice I've been given was, "If you never ask, you'll never know."

BIGGEST SUCCESS
Seeing culture change and diversity grow within the golf and fashion industry is probably the biggest success I've achieved so far. Of course, working with brands like Off-White, Oakley and Fear of God are incredible accomplishments, but I get the most joy out of seeing different cultures being brought together by a love of art and collaboration.

VALUES AND BELIEFS YOU NEED TO HAVE AS A PERSON TO BE A SUCCESS
I believe to be successful you must be eternally optimistic. Negativity surrounds us all, and if we choose to pay attention and listen to it, it can control us. Being optimistic and focusing on the positive truly makes anything possible. I also believe in spreading love and passion. Bring others around you and help the people who follow in your footsteps.

I think sometimes when we get to a certain level of achievement it's easy to forget where you came from. For me, the key to success is to

stay grounded and continue to be excited. We only have so much time, so be proud of who you are and where you come from. Then always be excited for what's next.

MY PASSION
I'm extremely passionate about playing golf! Additionally, I'm just as passionate about making sure that the youth coming up in the golf and fashion industry have a platform to be successful in a way I didn't have.

PARIS'S TIPS

- *I think social media is the most important tool of our generation. Young kids are now getting all their information and entertainment from social media. I think the more we can understand how to use these platforms, the more impactful they will become.*

- *Stay grounded and continue to be excited. We only have so much time, so be proud of who you are and where you come from and then always be excited for what's next.*

MARIANNA HEWITT

CO-FOUNDER, SUMMER FRIDAYS

TV host turned lifestyle blogger with a beauty focus, Marianna Hewitt has turned her beauty know-how into bestselling beauty brand Summer Fridays.

I always had a passion for sharing things with people and talking to people. When I was little, I would always get into trouble for talking in class! My teachers told my parents that I was always chatting, but my parents said it was a really good skill to have and I shouldn't have been scolded for that. It's certainly a skill that has helped me as an adult, and it has also helped me in my role as a TV host.

Growing up, I always wanted to be a television host. I wanted to share things with people and have a platform. I thought the only way to become one was to be like Oprah or Katie Couric! But then when the internet came around and there were platforms like blogging, YouTube and Instagram that were becoming more and more popular, I was able to pivot all of my favourite passions into a digital career.

STARTING OUT
Before I started my career in digital and beauty, I had a few different jobs. When I first moved to LA, I was an assistant in public relations. At the same time, I was a hostess at a sushi restaurant, because it's very expensive to live in LA.

What I really wanted to do was be a TV host, so I was fitting in auditions around my work schedule. I finally landed a job in television and did that for a few years – but then I started my YouTube channel and blog, which was another job in itself. And then I started my skincare line Summer Fridays.

SUMMER FRIDAYS
Lauren Gores Ireland is my co-founder of Summer Fridays, and the two of us have a huge passion for wellness, clean skincare and beauty products in general. We really loved the idea of melding our two worlds together. Lauren loves wellness, clean beauty and she's so healthy and really inspires me. She's taught me a lot about clean ingredients and what to put in my body (and what not to put in my body!), and that all goes into our skincare brand.

I took my love of luxury beauty, beauty products and being an educated consumer, and we merged our two passions together. We really wanted to create fast, effective products that had clean ingredients, while using our platforms as digital influencers to make products that our communities were asking for.

In the next five years, I can see us continuing to expand the brand, make more products globally and create more products inspired by our communities.

BEING A POWERHOUSE
To me, being a Powerhouse means doing whatever it is you want to do in your life. It's not about following someone else's rule book or how other people do things in life or in business, but really just paving your own way and not being afraid to do things differently.

When Lauren and I launched Summer Fridays, I think we were Powerhouses because we launched the brand with just one product. There's definitely been brands out there that launch with just one product – but when we were looking

around, there weren't many skin or beauty brands that launched with a single product. It's high risk, high reward. Luckily for us, our Jetlag Mask really took off, so it worked out for us. But it's definitely not a typical way to launch a brand!

FEMALE EMPOWERMENT
Since Lauren and I launched Summer Fridays, we have had such an amazing group of women encouraging us and supporting us from all walks of life and businesses. They have been so kind and offered advice, and I think that is just a great show of where female empowerment is at because when some brands do well, all brands do well.

MY INSPIRATION
There are so many people who inspire me and who I look up to. I love Oprah, and I talk about her all the time, but the reality is that she really ignited my passion for sharing and inspiring other people. I also really admire my friends like Jen Atkin, Jessica Alba and Jamie Kern Lima: they've created amazing brands – not just beauty brands, but I really feel like they've created whole lifestyle brands, and those are the women who've really supported me along the way.

MOTTO
"Don't be afraid of being told no."

MARIANNA'S TIPS

- *Create products that you love.*

- *Create packaging that can be shared on social media. Especially for brands that are digitally native, a lot of customers will see you there first, so it's important your packaging is something that inspires people to post.*

- *Be open to change. Sometimes things turn about better than you first thought if you are open to change!*

HOFIT GOLAN

FASHION INFLUENCER

Queen of the red carpets, Hofit Golan is a fashion celebrity and icon. She is a three-time award-winning influencer by Forbes and a global phenomenon.

ENTERING THE FASHION INDUSTRY

I was producing a charity function at the Royal Albert Hall in London in 2003. I was looking for something to wear as I was presenting on stage in front of five thousand people. I didn't really know anything about fashion at that point. I was introduced to a designer, Scott Henshall, who was up and coming at the time. He agreed to lend me a dress for the event.

He ended up dressing me for all the events surrounding the main event. His dresses were so beautiful, I didn't want to give them back, so I approached him about how we could work together, and he said: "If you could do for me what you did for me at this event at the Royal Albert Hall, I'll give you half the company."

Long story short, we got a gig with Coca-Cola and I became his business partner. That was the beginning of a huge fashion journey. Eventually, we would have over 200 points of sale all across the United States, Europe and Japan. That was my first step into fashion.

THE CHALLENGES OF THE RED CARPET

My very first red carpets were with Scott Henshall with the purpose of promoting our own line. It was difficult because there was no social media at that time, so it was hard to get the name of the brand out to the publications.

The biggest challenge is choosing what to wear on the red carpet when you have so many choices. It's a luxury problem! I look for what is going to have the most impact on the red carpet and what is going to get the best reaction.

POWER OF SOCIAL MEDIA

Social media allows you to remove the middleman. Before that we needed a manager, an agent, a publisher. Today, you can build your own following; you are your own magazine. If people resonate with you and your message, then you can open every door on your own. Social media has become a game-changer!

SETBACKS
Setbacks are receiving negativity from other people. People don't want to see you succeed all the time. The hardest lesson to learn is that even some of your loved ones and your friends, who you think have your back, don't really want to see you happy or succeed. People project their own negativity, fears and self-consciousness onto you. You have to understand that the only person you should listen to is yourself. The only opinion that counts is yours. You have to stay true to yourself.

ADVICE FOR WOMEN
If you want it, you have to go and get it. If you don't ask, you will never have anything. You have to put yourself out there and let the world know what you want, because you never know who might be at the other end of the conversation and who might be able to open up the right door at the right time.

You have got to be tenacious and motivated and never stop or give up. Everything is possible, and today you have every tool you need to achieve the dreams you have. If you want to get into the industry, find your angle, find your strength.

Find your own uniqueness, your own voice and then go after it.

BIGGEST HIGHLIGHT
Winning Forbes Influencer of the year and Monaco Lifestyle influencer of the year were great moments for me. Right now I am shooting for the cover of *Vogue* and *L'Officiel* magazine.

ADVICE FOR SUCCESS
You need to have resilience, motivation, positive attitude and commitment. You need to be able to work hard. Even when you are at an event or party, you need to stay connected to who you are and not fall in with negative people. Stay strong and focused and be professional at achieving your goals.

CELIA WALDEN

BRITISH JOURNALIST, EDITOR-AT-LARGE, AUTHOR

Celia Walden is the US Editor-at-Large for the Daily Telegraph *and a best-selling author, with four published books. She has been a regular guest on US and UK TV shows such as* The Today Show, BBC Breakfast, Sky News, GMTV, GB News, Good Morning Britain *and* Lorraine.

I was obsessed with books from an early age. I grew up with two very rambunctious older brothers, so I would often creep away from all the noise to somewhere quiet and read. I knew I wanted to be a writer from the age of twelve, when I decided to write some (absolutely awful) poetry. I think my mum must have read me too many tragic love stories when I was little, because when I look at the poems now they're all very mournful!

TURNING POINT IN YOUR CAREER
Far too many women can feel like frauds – sometimes for their whole lives, and no matter how successful they are. I'd be lying if I said I still suffered from imposter syndrome, because at some point (admittedly later than it should have been) when I was writing for the Telegraph newspaper in the UK, I was helping out a young intern and realised that I could actually teach her a few things – that I did actually know all sorts of things about my craft.

WRITING THE THRILLER NOVEL, 'THE SQUARE'
I live in a gorgeous, leafy little square in London, and after I wrote my first thriller, *Payday*, I was contracted to write another within the year. The only problem was that we were in the middle of the pandemic, and I was stuck at home like everybody else, doing the same thing day-in, day-out.

Writers do need to observe life to be inspired! But life was... a wasteland. So I came up with the idea of a devious IT lady working in a leafy London square, who starts sleuthing around after a beautiful French influencer is found dead.

GROWING UP IN PARIS
I will always think of Paris as my home because French was my first language and many of the most influential books I read in my teenage years were French. Often, I forget a word in English and can only think of it in French.

QUALITIES FOR SUCCESS
Self-belief has got to be right up there, if not the number one thing. We've all seen people who are not the best in their fields reach the top simply because of the strength of that self-belief. And I don't mean that in a bad way, because if you don't believe in yourself, why should anyone else?

CHALLENGES
I remember sitting in a black cab in London reading the most terrible review of my first book and wanting to burst into tears. But there's something very liberating about your ultimate nightmare actually coming true.

LESSONS

That there really is "a special place in hell for women who don't help other women." And that however hard you try to please everyone, there will always be people who are determined to dislike you, so ditching the people-pleasing is a must.

CHALLENGES

I've faced the same challenges as every woman. I've been patronised and under-estimated. But I've also been incredibly lucky, so I can't pretend I've overcome enormous obstacles in my professional life.

DEFINING MOMENT

I think most novelists would agree that seeing your book on a shelf in a bookshop for the first time is pretty hard to beat.

INSPIRATION

Every time I read a great thriller or a great newspaper interview, I feel inspired.

LEGACY

I just want to write the kind of novels people ignore their spouses for.

CELIA'S ADVICE

- *Write every day, even if it's just a paragraph.*

- *Read other peoples' writings every day.*

- *Don't pretend to be something you're not or adopt opinions you don't really believe. You will always be found out.*

- *If you're nice and fair to the people you work with, they will always go above and beyond for you..*

RACHEL ZOE

FASHION DESIGNER, STYLIST, BUSINESSWOMAN

Rachel Zoe is a fashion designer and stylist who has dressed some of the most prominent women around the world.

I was raised by my extraordinary parents who were and remain today completely culture-obsessed and determined to keep my sister and me informed of the world around us and all of its beauty. From a very young age we were immersed in the worlds of art, music, ballet, theatre and fashion. We travelled often as a family and I was always very inspired by my surroundings and was drawn to beauty and glamour. I lived for playing dress up and would spend hours in my mother's closet layering jewellery and accessories and always put on red lipstick because it made me feel special. I cannot remember a time that I didn't want to look and feel glamorous!

CAREER PATH
I graduated from George Washington University with a Major in Psychology and Sociology. At the time, I didn't know what a stylist was and couldn't fathom that I could have a career in fashion. I got my first job through a family friend as a fashion editor at *YM* magazine making very little money. From my very first day on the job, I was completely obsessed with it and knew this is what I would do for the rest of my life and honestly would have done it for free.

PASSION FOR SUCCESS
My parents would tell you most definitely I have been this way forever. I always wanted to be better than people expected me to be in anything I've done in life whether it was sports as a child or in my career later in life. I come from a very strong, ambitious and hardworking family. I have always been influenced by my brilliant father who is a self-made entrepreneur who came from very little means. He built a very successful business while remaining kind a great leader to his team. My mother taught me to be fearless and opinionated and to fight for myself because no one else will. She also made me understand that I could do anything that boys could do -- while always staying glamorous.

ADVICE
For the younger generation, it's so important not to feel entitled. In today's environment, where social media can seemingly create overnight sensations, it's important to know that success still requires hard work and dedication. You have to be led by your passion for what you do; the success will come if you truly love your job because it should never feel like work! It is so important to surround yourself with positivity and people that lift you up. You have to recognise your professional strengths and weaknesses and hire people that balance you.

CAREER TURNING POINT
It was definitely a turning point in my career when people started to wonder who was behind certain celebrity looks on the red carpet or everyday street style. My intention as a stylist was always to be behind the scenes where I am still most comfortable. Once my name became more well-known many more business opportunities presented themselves.

When The Rachel Zoe Project debuted in 2008 and ran for 5 seasons, I was exposed to an even wider audience which ultimately gave me an invaluable platform to expand my brand.

CAREER HIGHLIGHTS
I love every part of what I do - from launching a media business, my ready-to-wear collection and the Box of Style while still being a stylist forever at my core. I feel like I continue to build a personal connection with my audience which I'm grateful for every day. Anything I do

is to continue to educate woman on how to live their best lives in the most confident and glamorous way.

BALANCING CAREER AND FAMILY

I believe that being a working mother is the most challenging part of my life to date. Some days are easier than others, but my priorities have definitely shifted. I now approach work in a healthier, and more efficient way.

I choose to focus on more high impact projects so I can have real quality time with my family. I try to be one hundred percent present whether it be with my children or my work, but the struggle is real, and I often feel guilty on either side.

CHALLENGES

When I first started out, my boss told me I was too nice to make it in the fashion industry! Since then, I have remained true to who I am, but have definitely developed a thicker skin because I've been disappointed by people close to me. It took me a while to realise that you don't need to be friends with everyone you work with, and not everyone has your best interest at heart. Contrary to that I have also made lifelong friends through my career and consider some members of my team as family.

ON STYLE

Style is ever-changing and always evolving. Trends will come and go but one should always have their own personal style that makes them feel their best. One of the biggest differences today is that there is a lot more freedom of expression. When I first started out there were a lot of fashion "rules" (i.e., no white after Labor Day, don't mix metals, patterns etc.). Now the days of "do's and don'ts" are over and men and women are encouraged to interpret fashion in their own unique way.

SUCCESS

Success is being inherently driven by passion. I have never looked at my job as work, and I believe that success comes from a true love for what you do.

MOTTO

No matter what I do in my career, the true DNA of our brand has always been to empower women to live a life of style. Whether it's through television, books, designing my Rachel Zoe ready to wear collection or curating the Box of Style, everything I do is an extension of that message. Fashion and style should never be intimidating or only for the wealthy or famous. Style can be achieved with very little effort and on any budget, I promise.

RACHEL'S ADVICE

- Don't try to be all things to all people, because it's actually not possible. Focus on staying true to who you are and the core mission of your brand. I believe success can come while still leading with kindness and positivity.

- Learn from every experience.

- Confidence comes with time, and your mistakes will lead to your biggest lessons.

- You should not try to second guess every decision you make.

- Stay true to the mission of one's brand and never make apologies for who you truly are.

- Always have a seat at the table and a strong voice even when you find yourself in a tough room.

BELIEVE IN YOURSELF, TRUST YOUR GUT AND SURROUND YOURSELF WITH LIKE-MINDED, KIND PEOPLE WHO BRING NEW PERSPECTIVE.

LAUREN BUSH

TASH OAKLEY

FOUNDER OF A BIKINI A DAY, MONDAY SWIMWEAR & MONDAY ACTIVE

Sporting one of the world's most envied bodies, Natasha Oakley has made a business out of wearing beautiful bikinis in beautiful destinations, creating a worldwide phenomenon with the first ever bikini blog, titled A Bikini A Day – run alongside best friend Devin Brugman – and spawning a swimwear and an activewear label coveted by fans across the world.

I created the "A Bikini A Day" blog with my best friend, Devin Brugman, in Los Angeles. We realised we had a serious obsession with swimwear and the life that surrounds it, and wanted to share it with the world. It was really a passion project, to begin with!

Before we started the blog, I had my own production company and was actually shooting swimwear campaigns in Hawaii and Los Angeles. I think we can attribute the professional quality of our images from the early days to the fact that both Devin and I had experience with photography.

BUILDING THE BRAND

People instantly took to the concept of A Bikini A Day – we found that there was something for everyone to relate to, whether it was the friendship between Devin and me, our travels, our entrepreneurism or our personal style. In 2012, it was a fairly new concept to be documenting your life professionally on Instagram, so there was naturally a huge interest in the consistent content we were creating. Our content was a reflection of our lifestyle, and I think people really just gravitated towards it for obvious reasons: because the beach and warm weather appeal to most people! Also, there wasn't (at that stage) any kind of online platform that was dedicated to showcasing the latest suits from our favourite swimwear brands. It's always beneficial to know how something looks on different body types before you purchase online, and we provided that.

We noticed pretty soon after A Bikini A Day started to gain followers that a lot of the young women who were following us were feeling inspired by the way we were comfortable in our own skin. It was a real eye-opener for us, and we loved that we were able to help girls feel more confident within themselves to be in a bikini on the beach – which can be a very daunting thing.

THE SUPPORT NETWORK

I have an amazing group of people in my life who are very supportive and understanding of my career. I grew up with parents who each owned their own businesses and provided me with insight into the world of entrepreneurialism. But actually, the fact that my best friend is also my business partner was the kind of help you can't pass up, the kind that doesn't come around too often. Devin was my moral support as well as my business partner – we make an amazing team, and it wouldn't have been the same without her.

I think the key to our success was that we were providing something that didn't exist yet. We found our niche without actually looking for one, within an industry that was just becoming a legitimate career path: blogging and social media. We worked really hard to pursue what we viewed as an extremely unique opportunity for ourselves at that point in our lives, so I think it was a combination of our effort and innovativeness that was the key to our success. The photos, the clothes, the destinations? Yes, these beautiful things really do exist in our lives, but we are extremely appreciative of every opportunity we are given and always have been. Even in the early days when we weren't travelling the world and being gifted by amazing designers, we felt like the luckiest girls in the world just for the simple fact that we were able to create our own career path.

A TYPICAL DAY

This is the million-dollar question! A typical workday for us varies from place to place, but our love for the beach definitely keeps us in check and on top of our game. The beach is our playground and our office, so when we're there, we make sure to shoot as much as we can.

It's a win-win! An average A Bikini A Day shoot includes around 50-60 bikinis in one day.

THE LABELS

Creating our own swimwear was a natural progression for us – wearing literally hundreds of suits a year gives you a pretty good idea of what's out there and what's missing. Monday Swimwear really is a product of our environment. We wanted to design suits that had longevity, were classic, timeless pieces and were made for all figures. Monday Active was born of the same concept.

Activewear should be comfortable, supportive and stylish in order for women to feel confident when they're working out. Monday Swimwear and Active share the same notion aesthetically, which is important for us so our friends and followers know what to expect across the board from our brands.

Our biggest hurdles are conceptualising these designs without sacrificing style, quality or comfort – but we think we do a pretty great job! Apart from that, we have had to learn the ins and outs of an industry that was completely new to us; we do not have partners in our brand, so every aspect of the business is managed by us: the design, production, manufacturing, e-commerce sites, etc.

THE CONTROVERSY

I was taken aback when the issue of airbrushing dropped in the media as I was completely misquoted. The question I had been confronted with in the interview was, "Why do you think social media influencers are editing their images?" My response was, "I think people are trying to mimic what they see in the media." It was quite satirical how my words got twisted in that interview and apparently became an "admission" – but I really wasn't threatened by it. My business is bikinis. I'm in a swimsuit 90% of the year, attend appearances all over the world, conduct photoshoots weekly, etc... There is nothing my photographs can say about myself or my body that people don't see in reality. I felt so supported during that time, and I knew the only opinions that mattered were of the people who knew me, like my friends and followers.

In terms of feeling the pressure to look the part – looking good and feeling good are one in the same, really. I feel better in all aspects of my life when I'm working out consistently. It's challenging to find time, which is why I opt for HIIT (High-Intensity Interval Training) workouts that suit my busy schedule, and it makes all the difference to my energy levels – I'm not sure I could lead such a hectic lifestyle without the energy I gain from training. There is obviously pressure in the media and online to always look your best, but it doesn't affect me negatively. I'm not afraid of criticism; I have a pretty thick skin, which is important in this industry. I just make sure I am doing what I know is best for me, and it seems to work in my favour. So yes, I do encourage people to do the same in that respect.

COLLABORATIONS

I have to be selective with the brands and companies I collaborate with because the nature of my work means it is a direct reflection of my personality and beliefs. I am approached by a huge number of brands every week! But the truth is, my schedule is crazy; I live between three major cities and travel at least 80% of the year. Aside from choosing brands that reflect my own style and are in line with my own brand both aesthetically and morally, I have to coordinate any collaborations according to my schedule. If there were three more of me, I could potentially look at working with all of my most loved brands!

My favourite collaboration so far is actually the collection I designed for GUESS. The collection itself was inspired by vintage GUESS swimwear worn by the likes of Claudia Schiffer and Anna Nicole Smith, and the campaign was shot in black and white, true to some of the most iconic GUESS photo shoots.

THE CHALLENGES

Deciding how much is too much when it comes to business is probably my biggest challenge. I'm very passionate about my business and I find it difficult to switch off. I think most people who have a business of their own or any kind of passion would feel the same way. My business is like my baby – I want to make sure I'm nurturing it in every way I can and helping it to grow and be successful, which requires me to be on the clock at all hours of the day and night. My situation of running the business as well as being the face of it is extremely unique – I am solely responsible for my own success and there is no one that can take my place in that position.

And fitting everything in! I have to select jobs according to my schedule and locations throughout the year. I have jobs lined up over the next couple of years, so it can definitely feel overwhelming at times. Unfortunately, I do have to turn down jobs quite often, but I have to be conscious to not 'spread myself too thin', as the saying goes. I commit myself fully to the jobs and collaborations I take on and want to make sure I can always perform to the best of my ability.

TASH'S TIPS

- *Remain true to yourself. I know it's cliché and maybe even overstated, but it's completely true. People are attracted to authenticity and can very easily sense when someone is not necessarily passionate about what they are sharing with the world.*

HOPE. THERE IS ALWAYS LIGHT AT THE END OF THE TUNNEL.

NOVLENE MILLS

INDIA HICKS

FOUNDER & CREATIVE DIRECTOR AT INDIA HICKS INC.

India Hicks is a former model, the bestselling author of three books and the daughter of David Hicks, one of the world's most celebrated interior designers. She founded her eponymous lifestyle brand India Hicks Inc. in 2015, which encompasses a range of accessories and fragrances. She is passionate about inspiring women to follow their dreams.

The major driving force for me is the belief in what I'm doing. I had two unique parents who led individual lives; both influenced me to think independently, although I don't think they anticipated I would be the founder of a direct sales company. Or move to an island. Or have five children. Or not learn to speak French with a proper accent!

I started modelling quite late – when I was 19 years old. Most models start much younger now. I once drove down to the countryside with a guest of my father's who happened to be a journalist working for *W Magazine*. He had come to interview my father about his famous garden and ended up inviting me to be a part of a story called "New Beauties". Ralph Lauren spotted me in this feature and flew me, first class, to California for my first Ralph Lauren job. There were flowers in my room and a warm welcome. From that modelling job, I went to a Winnebago in Florida in 103 degrees, doing 40 shots a day for some dreadful German catalogue, and I realised the real world of modelling was not all like the Ralph Lauren world of modelling.

ENTERING THE WORLD OF INTERIOR DESIGN

Living under the imposing eye of (my father) David Hicks, I was always a little bit tentative about the world of interior design and finding my own voice. It was only when I moved to a small island in the middle of an ocean and bought our home, Hibiscus Hill, that I was brave enough to decorate it in my own way and not mimic my father. When a hurricane destroyed a small hotel on the island a few months later, I offered to redecorate and relaunch it, which I did with my other half, David. This project caught quite a lot of media attention and gave me the confidence to really start designing on many different levels and in all sorts of categories.

INDIA HICKS INC.

Having had a wonderful licensing career in partnership with other companies, I decided it was time to do something that I could truly own for myself. I designed the collections to be beautifully crafted and also to tell the stories of my life, and the rather mad moments in it. My two partners (because you always need partners in crime) and I knew that those stories might get lost on the cold, hard shelves of retailers. Instead, we chose to build the business by partnering with like-minded women who adore the design world and were looking for a new chapter to their own story. I never imagined myself in the world of direct sales, but now I can't imagine myself anywhere else.

THE INSPIRATIONS

My collections are inspired by my British heritage, my island life and some madcap daydreams. I drew from different stories, moments, absurd adventures and unusual characters I have met, most of whom I am related to! These stories bring the products to life.

I don't have one particular mentor, but I've been inspired by many outstanding people along the way.

The partners I mentioned, who have been embedded in the world of business for a long time, shaped the way our company was created and continue to guide me every day. And, of course, I look to women who have set an example by believing in themselves and being passionate about what they do, whether it's writing poetry or managing a hedge fund.

The biggest challenge in my business so far is being taken seriously. Coming from a background where it wasn't necessarily expected for me to work and being a woman in the workplace were the two main things I had to negotiate. The key to success and longevity is continuously moving forward and never giving up. It certainly isn't easy.

My advice to aspiring entrepreneurs is to get advice. Listen to others. Learn from your mistakes. But always go with your gut.

INDIA'S TIPS

- *Act appropriately (which will make some people who know me well laugh because I swear like a sailor and have the humour of a twelve-year-old).*

- *Dress appropriately.*

- *Be the person you hope your daughter looks up to.*

- *Don't be scared by social media. But don't be controlled by it either.*

- *And never take a miniature dog into a business meeting.*

AERIN LAUDER

FOUNDER AND CREATIVE DIRECTOR OF AERIN

The granddaughter of Estée Lauder, Aerin Lauder has always been surrounded by cosmetics, makeup and fragrance. Her own passion for the industry grew after spending her summers working for the family business, where she still acts as Style and Image Director. This led her to create her own beauty and fragrance collection, AERIN, in 2012, expanding to home and accessories.

Beauty and fragrance are my heritage and my passion. For as long as I can remember, I've been surrounded by it and completely enthralled by it: it's part of me.

When I was in sixth grade, I went to school with all my new lip glosses. Everyone wanted to try them on, and I knew then that this was something people really wanted. For fragrance, I remember getting into the car with my grandmother, Estée Lauder, and being aware of her scent. She was always testing different fragrances, but she especially loved the fragrance "Beautiful". We both shared a passion for flowers, especially roses.

ESTÉE LAUDER

Estée was an amazing grandmother and friend. She was also an incredible role model and taught me the importance of passion, style, hard work, family and, of course, all things beautiful. She taught me so much and has definitely inspired the person I am today – as both a mother and a businesswoman. She taught me the importance of quality and attention to detail and, above all, the value of customer relationships. We also both share a love of roses, beauty and fragrance – things my grandmother shared with me from a very young age.

Her biggest strength was her passion. She was unique because although so many women are driven and passionate, they are not always feminine. She taught me the importance of being feminine and strong. She would always have perfect lipstick, and she was brilliant at marketing. She really connected with her consumers, which is so important, and this was what really set her and the brand apart. She would always say, "A woman knows what a woman wants."

KEEPING IT IN THE FAMILY

I think it's important to surround yourself with people who care about you and who you care about, and working with family is just that. My family supports me but also pushes me to always think ahead and do better. Family can also be very honest, which can be hard, but it is important to know what people really think when creating products.

I spent my summers during college working for the family business, then began my career with the Estée Lauder companies in 1992 as a member of the Prescriptives marketing team, working across programs for the colour, fragrance and skincare businesses.

Today, I'm the Style and Image Director for the Estée Lauder brand as well as the founder and Creative Director of AERIN. Some of the most important initiatives during my time as Creative Director of Estée Lauder included launching the Sensuous campaign, the first of its kind to include multiple models with Gwyneth Paltrow, Hilary Rhoda, Carolyn Murphy and Elizabeth Hurley. This was a concept that Estée Lauder had never done before and was one of the most successful to date. In 2010, we introduced Liu Wen as the first Asian spokesmodel for the brand, making beauty history,

and we collaborated with Tom Ford to relaunch one of Estée's most brilliant fragrances, Youth Dew.

The biggest lesson I learnt was the importance of finding the balance between work and life. Estée was the first person to teach me how important it is to be passionate and proud of what you do, and she always talked about balance. She was so ahead of her time in that she had a career and a family, but always managed to take time out for herself. So that's what I try and do every day.

CREATING AERIN
I am fortunate to have learned so much from a lifetime in beauty. The time came for me to take those lessons and re-interpret them and pursue my own vision, from my own perspective. AERIN has been an amazing journey. I started the brand in 2012, and it has been the perfect way for me to explore different ways to expand the modern woman's lifestyle and provide the product she needs – from beauty and fashion to lifestyle and home.

I was always being asked what was in my makeup bag, and I felt there was a void in the marketplace for a feminine, effortless beauty brand. This was really what inspired me to create the AERIN Beauty brand. I wanted to explore different ways to expand the modern woman's lifestyle and provide the product she needs – from beauty and fashion to lifestyle and home. I feel very strongly about every product the AERIN brand makes and love to be involved from start to finish. It's my name on the package, so I want to make sure it's perfect. My grandmother felt the same way, so that's definitely a drive I got from her.

AERIN Beauty is a luxury lifestyle beauty and fragrance brand inspired by effortless style. It is designed for and inspired by women with classic, effortless style, but always with a modern point of view. AERIN Beauty allows women to embrace being feminine and pretty through a curated wardrobe of fragrances and rose essentials that are very personal to the woman who is wearing them.

The AERIN Fragrance Collection is really an expression of my life, my memories and my travels. Whether it's a floral note with a fabulous musk or the idea of something that evokes fresh air and sun with a tropical floral, the combinations are unique and distinctive. My hope is that women can select a scent that evokes their own special memories or experiences.

With the AERIN Rose Cologne Collection, I wanted to share three different rose notes I have enjoyed throughout my life in a collection of scents which offer a lighter, luxurious fragrance for every day, every mood and for any reason. Each fragrance embodies my love of roses in a different way. Bamboo Rose is inspired by the more formal gardens you see in Japan. Garden Rose is my way of capturing the lively and lush garden roses you see in the English countryside. Linen Rose brings me to summers past – back to the Eastern shores of Long Island. Each is tied to a very specific memory, and I experience each memory every time I smell each cologne.

The packaging is inspired by natural elements such as stones and flowers. Each fragrance bottle has a different gem in a pretty and soft pastel shade and includes golden details carefully selected to reflect the spirit of the fragrance. Each carton features an exclusive print design.

THE CHALLENGES AND SUCCESSES
Balancing everything is one of my biggest challenges – just like other working mothers. It's so important to always try and take time for yourself. If you are happy, everyone around you will be happy. Success is feeling proud and passionate about what you do every day.

The values of hard work and determination were instilled in me from a very young age. I was always taught that these two elements are integral to having not only a successful business but a successful life. I am really proud when someone tells me they love my products.

Everything we create is a result of a long process, so it needs to be extraordinary. And I'm constantly working on new projects and new collaborations that will expand the AERIN brand. I look forward to evolving the future collections with inspiration from my travels.

AERIN'S TIPS

- *Hard work and determination.*

- *If you are happy, everyone around you will be happy.*

- *Success is feeling proud and passionate about what you do each day.*

LAURA GALLON

JEWELLERY DESIGNER

French jewellery designer Laura Gallon combines personal expression, family heritage and savoir-faire to create timeless pieces that have been worn at the Cannes Film Festival.

I was born in Paris in July of 1989, two hundred years after the French Revolution! My parents remember the city being extremely busy with the celebration of the anniversary, which made it almost impossible to reach the hospital for my birth. My father was a renowned dental surgeon, and my mother was a flight attendant on the Concorde plane. They met on a plane (of course!). We lived just outside of Paris in a village called Marnes-La-Coquette, which was very charming and peaceful while having the advantage of being very close to Paris. I've been travelling for as long as I can remember. Actually, I was only three months old when I went on a plane for the first time. We had a house in South Carolina where we would go for vacations, so I grew up between France and the United States.

CAREER BEGINNINGS
One day, my father gave me a pair of fan-shaped diamond and platinum earrings that his grandfather had made for his wife in the 1920s. His grandfather, Georges Gallon, was a renowned jeweller in Orléans, two hours south of Paris. My father was born in the jewellery workshop (back in the days when home births were common) and was raised by his grandparents. Holding the earrings in my hands and seeing how beautiful they were, I realised the magnitude of my family's jewellery heritage. That's when I decided to become a gemmologist and revive the family business.

LAUNCH OF THE COLLECTION
I started my company in May 2020, at the beginning of the pandemic. After obtaining my gemmologist certification from GIA, I worked for a jewellery workshop in Los Angeles. The workshop closed its doors for the pandemic, and no one knew for how long. I found myself with a lot of free time on my hands, which gave me the opportunity to start sketching pieces inspired by gemstones that I had acquired at trade shows.

INSPIRATION
Most of my designs are inspired by the creative DNA of my great grandfather's work, so it has an Art Deco feel with a modern touch. In terms of metals, I work with gold and platinum and use a lot of different natural gemstones. Being a gemmologist, I place gemstones at the heart of my creations and hand-select each one of them. I work with diamonds, rubies, sapphires and emeralds but also enjoy introducing my clients to lesser-known gems such as spinels, tsavorites, tanzanites or rhodolite garnets. I've been very lucky to have two incredible role models who raised me. My parents were both incredibly passionate and fulfilled by their respective careers, which is something I've been yearning to find for myself. Then, I've had some great mentors in my profession who have been kind enough not only to share their knowledge but also to welcome me with open arms into the industry. I'm thinking of my friend Dave Bindra, who is one of the world's best gem dealers.

CHALLENGES
Before discovering my passion for jewellery, I struggled quite a lot to find a career path. I started working in the fashion industry after attending the Parsons School of Design in New York City. I worked for different high-end companies but felt very disconnected from the mentality of the people I was

encountering. I then tried to work in luxury hospitality but was missing the creative aspect. From there, I also tried events management but didn't feel fulfilled either. At this point, I felt like I would never find my path. I felt like all my friends had stable careers and were building something while I would never find my purpose. However, I never accepted to settle for something that felt wrong. I always listened to my gut feeling. When my father gave me the earrings, I didn't get scared to explore this new, unknown path. So, I think that this is how I got through it: listening to my gut feeling and not being scared to start over.

QUALITIES FOR SUCCESS
Determination, social skills (making contacts and knowing how to use them), luck and a good story. Knowing how to sell yourself is key, whichever industry you are in.

FUTURE ASPIRATIONS
This year is a very exciting one! I've been invited, along with other high jewellery brands, to design a one-of-a-kind piece featuring the rare and stunning gemstone Paraiba Tourmaline to be featured in a coffee table book which will be presented at the Ritz in Paris during Fashion Week. I'm also in the process of designing my upcoming collection entitled "Dynasty", which is inspired by a bracelet made by my great-grandfather that we were lucky to buy at auction at the end of last year. This collection will be my best work so far, paying tribute to the Gallon Dynasty. And finally, I'm working on introducing the brand into new markets such as Mexico.

LEGACY
I want to be remembered as the woman who woke up a sleeping beauty (my family's brand) and turned it into a successful international business. The style of jewellery that my family has been making for over 100 years is truly timeless, so I want people to desire it, recognise it and wear it forever.

LAURA'S ADVICE

- *Be passionate about it because, like any other career, it's not an easy one, and if you are not truly passionate about it, you won't enjoy the process and will end up giving up when it gets hard.*

- *Meet as many people as you can, connect, get involved, ask questions – you will learn a lot and make valuable connections which will serve you down the line.*

- *Don't be scared to fail, because it's the only way to learn and it's all part of your journey.*

- *Go to as many trade shows and industry events as possible; what you learn in a classroom is a great start, but you will learn so much more on the ground.*

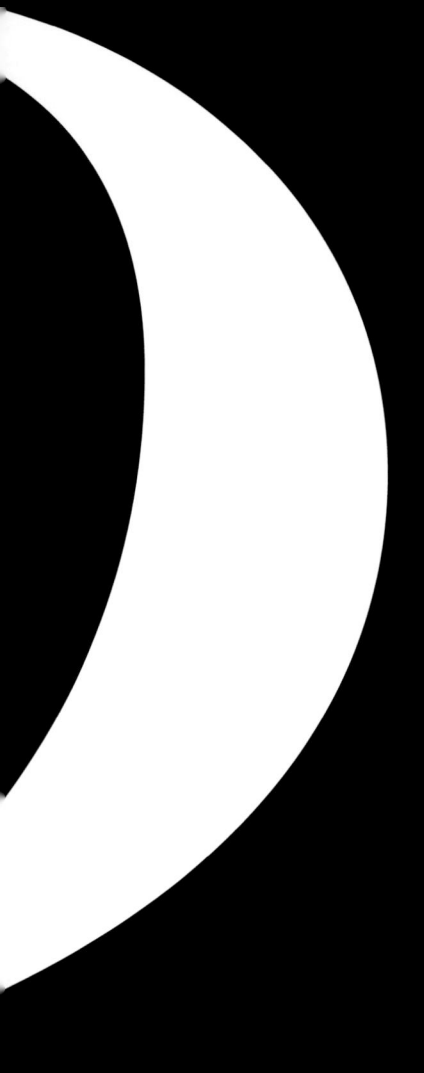

PEOPLE DO MAKE THEIR LUCK BY DARING TO FOLLOW THEIR INSTINCTS, TAKING RISKS, AND EMBRACING EVERY POSSIBILITY.

ESTÉE LAUDER

JO MALONE

FOUNDER OF JO LOVES

Jo Malone is a pioneer in the fragrance industry, creating her eponymous line of fragrances, luring a cult-like following of customers in the mid-1990s before selling to Estée Lauder. In 2011, she launched Jo Loves, designed to capture the inspirations in Jo's life.

I think everybody has something in life that they are really good at. There are lots of things I can't do, but I have an amazing sense of smell. Everything I see translates into smell: I see colour in smell, I hear music in smell … basically for me, everything translates into fragrance notes. It's like a language for my nose.

Ever since I was a 10-year-old girl, I would experiment with different smells, mixing oils and flowers from my garden on my stove to learn how they worked together.

I started out my career as a beauty therapist at age 22, doing facials from my tiny apartment in London, where I was running around in a little white coat. We didn't have a penny to rub together, so all I had was a massage bed. I had no actual bed in my apartment, just a blue foam mattress that I would put away during the day, and bring out at night. We had no furniture either, but I was able to transform this tiny little place into a spa that clients seemed to love.

HUMBLE BEGINNINGS

I started off with a dozen clients. They would climb three flights of stairs to my little salon, where they would have their face done. I wanted to make my own face cream, so I started mixing oils that I had made in Paris to use on the women. In the early days, I would experiment with essential oils, including jojoba, avocado, rosemary…

The business took off when I created a nutmeg and ginger body lotion that I would give to clients as a gift, and the women loved it! I was massaging people's arms with it after their facials, and everyone wanted to buy the body lotion. Twelve clients grew to 20 clients within a week through word of mouth. I didn't have money for a bed, let alone advertising and marketing, but I started getting the beauty editors of major magazines through, and that is primarily how word spread.

Kathy Phillips, who was the fashion director of *Tatler* magazine, wanted to write an article about me – and that was the start of something unbelievable. The article was titled, 'Scenter of the Universe' and created such a buzz and demand that when we opened up our first store in October 1994, there was a line around the block.

From there, newspapers across the country wanted to write about us: the *Financial Times* and *British Vogue* … and the demand grew and grew for the products that I had invented in my tiny little kitchen. And it wasn't just in the UK – the whole world wanted them!

The original packaging was very simple – just little plastic bottles. I would go down to a little warehouse and pick up six crates of boxes filled with bottles, create little labels on the typewriter and go down to the local printer to get them printed. I would give each product out in little white Chinese takeaway boxes. The orders began to pour in, and that was the moment I knew that the Jo Malone brand was about to take off. From there, we just grew and grew.

SELLING JO MALONE LONDON
Often, businesses reach a point where they grow so rapidly that you can feel it backfiring. Within five years of opening our first store, we sold the business to Estée Lauder. When people ask me why I sold the business, I tell them that growth can start to backfire. So I was looking for a company with deep pockets, distribution and heart – I needed someone who really loved me and loved the industry. I could find the first two – money and distribution – but it's that last ingredient – the heart – that completes the triangle for growth.

I met Leonard Lauder in 1999, and when I signed a deal to hand Jo Malone London over, I honestly thought I was going to stay with the company forever. It was just a happy time. But 18 months into it, I was diagnosed with breast cancer. And that changed everything for me. I was given a very poor diagnosis and told that I didn't have that long. I had to have surgery, so I decided to go to America and live for a year in New York, fighting the cancer. I came out a very different person. I felt I didn't belong in the company anymore. And so I exited in 2006.

When I left Estée Lauder in 2006, I knew I had made a huge mistake. I remember that last moment, putting the last bottle on the shelf and turning the key in the door. It was announced in the press, and it was too late to say that I had changed my mind. This is a huge lesson to myself and others – that sometimes we make big mistakes, but it doesn't mean to say you can't go on and still fulfil your dreams. I had agreed to a five-year lockout – but as a creator and artist, the thought of not creating anything in five years was probably one of the worst things I had done for myself. So much so that for a couple of years, I wouldn't even walk through a cosmetics store – it was just too emotional!

Then, one day, I was walking through Harrods, and I opened a jar of a beauty product and smelt it, and I felt tears welling up in my eyes. I knew I would have to go back to the industry. I tried to write myself a CV, but mine was just so awful. I felt so humiliated. I didn't know who to call for someone to give me a job. I would have done anything in the cosmetics industry, but I just had no confidence. I lost who Jo Malone was: the spirit of Jo. And I was so unhappy.

CREATING "JO LOVES"
When the five-year lockout came to an end, I thought I was going to make television. So I created a reality television show called *High Street Dreams*, about entrepreneurs. For one of the episodes, I was standing with a family filling bottles of chilli sauce at their home, and I had a white coat on and a hair net – and I think it was filling the bottles and seeing this family's passion and the reminder of the original white coat I used to wear, that I just knew then and there that I just had to try one more time in the industry I was so passionate about.

At that moment it wasn't about building a global brand – just about doing something that I was passionate about and that I loved. A few days later, as I sat around a kitchen table, I wondered what it would mean if I did it all again. So I put together a concept, went to the head counsel of Estée Lauder and showed them so they didn't get any surprises, and then sat down and worked out what I was going to do next.

In 2011, I launched Jo Loves. It was hard work! At first, I got the packaging wrong, and I got the fragrances wrong. It's really important for people to understand that despite entrepreneurs looking like they get it right the first time, they often get it wrong. But they push till they get it right. And that's exactly what I did. Now I am so proud that I did: I look at this brand and I am so proud of it.

The Jo Loves Pomelo fragrance was our first fragrance, and it symbolised to me that I could do this again. It is the hope of another chapter in my life, and it is a symbol to me that my dream of changing the world with fragrance is very much alive.

THE LAUNCH

We started Jo Loves in a studio by invitation only – and I was so surprised about the number of people wandering around trying to find the studio! We then did a pop-up shop in Selfridges. We had created a hunger around the brand: and there was an ever-growing tribe that spread the message to help make the brand strong and powerful, so people are driven into department stores saying they want it. That's now happening in the Middle East, New York, China, Mumbai, India and all over America. Net-a-Porter has helped spread the word, too. They have those qualities I was talking about before: distribution, deep pockets and heart. They were able to take our brand and put it into the hands of people with whom we share the same market and clientele as Jo Loves. Emirates Airlines has also been a huge supporter, promoting the product in its duty-free line. Next we will be changing the way the world wears fragrance.

WHAT MAKES JO A GAME CHANGER

"I'm not frightened of being the only one standing that believes in my dream. I will stand alone if I have to."

JO'S TIPS

- *Success is about 10 per cent inspiration and 90 per cent perspiration.*

- *Fix your mind on your goal. Every single day, the world changes, and people change. Head towards your dream.*

- *When you fall down and fail, pick yourself back up and start walking towards your goal. You have to have the motivation.*

- *Enjoy the journey.*

- *When you have succeeded – don't forget to think to yourself how lucky you are.*

- *Don't think you're owed it, but that you've earned it and it's your right.*

PAULA BREZAVSCEK

FOUNDER OF AZALA SKIN CLINIC, MIAMI

Paula Brezavscek's skills as a physician associate have been employed by clients from Victoria's Secret models, actors, singers, musicians and supermodels such as Elle MacPherson. She is the daughter of first-generation immigrants, born and raised in a Spanish enclave of New Jersey.

My mother was born in the Basque region of northern Spain. She was forced to leave Spain after the Spanish Civil War in search of new opportunities and ended up working as an au pair in New York City. She eventually found a position as a seamstress for a fashion house, creating unique haute couture pieces. My father, whose parents fled Northern Italy before World War II, was born and raised in Buenos Aires, Argentina. He came to the United States as a young adult in search of the American dream and met my mother in New York City. Soon after my parents were married, my mother gave birth to a baby girl who arrived several months early and, unfortunately, with a hearing impairment. As I grew up alongside my sister, I watched how the world treated her and others with disabilities differently, and was deeply disappointed in the broken system that had failed us. Around the same time, my mother picked up a job at a nursing home. I spent countless hours watching her tenderly care for the elderly patients with such patience and warmth. I remember these experiences with an acute sense of sadness, but they taught me the importance of treating all people with respect and kindness. In an effort to help my sister, my parents enrolled my sister in horseback riding lessons designed to assist those with disabilities. I watched her lessons as a two-year-old with wide eyes and a pounding heart, and instantly fell in love with horses. It became a life-long passion. As an adolescent, my life revolved around being an avid equestrian. When I was in the saddle, the world seemed to stop, and all that existed in the steaming early morning rides were the pounding of hoofbeats, the sting of the leather bridle in my hands, the feeling of flight. I competed in horse shows, jumping, dressage, combined training, and thoroughbred racing. Riding ultimately led me to Cornell University, where I competed at the collegiate level as a member of the varsity equestrian team. At Cornell, I began to focus on my academic goals and naturally gravitated towards science and medicine I was fascinated by Nutritional Sciences, which seemed to be one of the most important underlying factors in preventing disease. During my graduate studies to obtain a master's degree in clinical medical sciences, I discovered dermatology. I had sported facial acne since the age of 25, and like many adolescents, experienced the conflict that arises when one's appearance does not exactly match up to their expectations. I decided to specialize in dermatology, because in a world that is often times unfair and broken, skin issues were one thing that I could fix.

CAREER BEGINNINGS

Throughout my childhood, adolescence, and collegiate life, I had a passion for art and was always enrolled in art classes, whether it was ceramics, pointillism painting, sketching with graphite pencils, photography, or woodworking. I loved hiking and mountain climbing, and travelled the world to visit Buddhist temples. I loved discovering new things and working with my hands and bringing projects to life. Being a perfectionist, I would obsess over any details or imperfections in my work, making me reluctant to showcase them during exhibitions. Realising this wasn't a sustainable quality for an artist, I decided to pursue a career in medicine, which provided stability and allowed me to continue art as a hobby. It wasn't until I was practicing as a licensed physician assistant in clinical dermatology that I found my unique talent. Understanding the scientific process of what is happening to our bones, muscle, and skin as we age, and understanding the properties of these "fillers" and medical devices that were being used to address ageing, this practice of cosmetic dermatology or aesthetic medicine seemed a natural progression.

LAUNCH OF AZALA SKIN CLINIC

For many years I practised clinical dermatology in Miami, treating skin cancers and excising tumours and cysts. After mastering the clinical practice of dermatology, I decided to refocus my career on aesthetic dermatology. I opened Azala Skin Clinic, a luxury medical spa focused on sustainable ageing. I aimed to create a safe space for clients to receive education and treatments, utilising cutting-edge technology to restore skin, strengthen specific muscles, and perform injectable artistry, all of which are designed to allow my patients to age gracefully with beauty, confidence and dignity.

CHALLENGES

The biggest challenge for me has always been balancing work and family. Both of my parents have had major health issues, and my sister continues to live with a hearing disability. Handling end-of-life issues with parents is incredibly difficult, but I remember how my mother cared for her patients in the nursing home with such kindness and patience. I remember how hard my father worked to support us. I remember my sister learning how to read lips and communicate in a world that would forever be silent for her. All of these experiences gave me the strength and fortitude to carry my family, my business, and my daughter through difficult times.

MOST POPULAR TREATMENTS FOR WOMEN

Radio frequency microneedling treatments like Morpheus 8 and Exion are popular for tightening skin on the face and body. Emsculpt and Emsella devices, which strengthen muscles, have also gained traction. These are particularly beneficial for postpartum women, improving rectus diastasis (separation of the abdominal muscles), strengthening pelvic floor muscles, and inducing collagen to help women regain their pre-baby bodies. My most popular treatments are injectables, my specialty, to restore youthfulness. I use filler injections to address bone changes, provide structural support, and reposition tissues; neurotoxin injections to lift the face and neck; and biostimulators to improve skin texture and composition. Utilising the latest advancements in aesthetic medical devices minimises the number of injectables needed by addressing all aspects of ageing synergistically.

CELEBRITY CLIENTS

I also am so grateful to the beautiful and entrepreneurial Elle Macpherson, who has graced many fashion runways, magazine covers, and TV screens for years and continues to do so. Not only does she trust in me to help her maintain that glowy skin, but she graciously included me and my skin clinic in articles written about her beauty routine. I have been very blessed to have many models, Victoria Secret's Angels, journalists, politicians, judges, actors, singers, musicians, celebrity chefs, artists and even NBA and NFL athletes come sit in my chair, but due to the nature of my business, I prefer not to tell all!

FAVOURITE TREATMENT

My favourite treatment for women is when they come in for facial restoration, specifically someone who has never had any previous fillers. For me this is the perfect fresh canvas, so I can utilise my injection techniques to restore her to her youthful self. If I have to pick a specific area of injectables that are my favourite, it would be lips (or perioral restoration). I guess this is my favourite because I think there are a lot of bad lip injections being done out there, and when done properly, no one should be able to tell unless there is a significant augmentation.

LEGACY

My joy in my professional life is helping others, whether directly within my aesthetics practice or through teaching. Understanding the uniqueness of each patient is crucial. Taking the time to get to know your patients and understanding their goals is essential.

PAULA'S ADVICE

- *You need to have a dream, ambition, and the courage to take initiative; be diligent, determined, receptive to constructive criticism, and surround yourself with a great social support system.*

- *If you haven't taken art classes, please do. This allows you to understand how shadows and light will play upon your canvas.*

- *Beauty and individuality should be timeless; trends aren't always great for every person.*

- *Take the time to listen. A lot of times, other things are happening in people's lives and the frustration could be manifesting itself on a wrinkle, where whatever you do may not make them happy if you haven't addressed or made them aware of the underlying problem.*

- *Climb mountains, start your own business, and change the world.*

*DREAMING
AFTER ALL
IS A FORM OF
PLANNING.*

GLORIA STEINEM

KATHRYN EISMAN

TELEVISION HOST, *UNDRESSED WITH KATHRYN EISMAN*
AUTHOR, FOUNDER, HIGH HEEL JUNGLE

One of the most celebrated TV hosts and New York Times best-selling author, Kathryn Eisman is a worldwide phenomenon with a global lifestyle brand: High Heel Jungle.

ENTERING THE FASHION INDUSTRY

My passion for fashion began as a young girl. I remember sleeping in my first pair of Italian leather shoes and just staring at them as a thing of beauty!

When I was seventeen, Marion Hume, the legendary fashion journalist and then Editor-in-Chief of *Vogue Australia*, moved in next door. I had just started modelling, and she and her husband would invite me over for tea (and a glass of wine when I turned 18), and we would talk about life and fashion and things like the Avant-Garde movement. It was like a new world was opening up for me,

I started modelling in Sydney. My first ever job was for David Jones, which now stocks my hosiery label, High Heel Jungle.

While I enjoyed modelling for its access, I always preferred the journalistic aspect of fashion much more than having a voice. Writing and discussing what clothing said about us as people and society was more interesting than being photographed. I studied Communications Journalism in Sydney, and while I was studying, I wrote my first book, *How To Tell a Man by His Shoes*, exploring the comical and yet uncannily accurate link between what we wear and who we truly are. I realised I had this sixth sense doing 'wardrobe readings', decoding the essence of someone based on their subconscious and conscious wardrobe choices. The book became an international bestseller, and I moved to New York for the launch. My first TV appearance was for ABC's *TODAY* show, and I was hired as the youngest on-air reporter for NBC. It was heaven: hard but magic.

In the role, I got to interview presidents and world leaders and head our coverage for New York Fashion Week backstage with the greats like Oscar de la Renta, Carolina Herrera, and Diane von Furstenberg. I later moved to Los Angeles to head Fashion and Lifestyle coverage for *E! News*. In that role, I would predict and cover the latest fashion and cultural trends and interview everyone from the Kardashians to Taylor Swift. I loved creating stories that peeled back the layers to see how trends and pop culture icons are created. I covered Kendall Jenner and Hailey Beiber's first New York fashion week as they practised their walk. I had one-on-ones with Selena Gomez and Taylor Swift. I also wrote my second book, *How To Tell a Woman by Her Handbag* and toured the world talking about the psychology of style.

CAREER HIGHLIGHTS

It's been rewarding having multiple Emmy Award Nominations at E! But the stars truly aligned when I returned to Sydney to co-executive-produce and host a new fashion show, *Undressed with Kathryn Eisman*, for Paramount Plus and Channel Ten with Bruna Papandrea, Eden Gaha and Made Up Stories. The television series combines the beauty and production value of premium dramas with the raw truth of reality TV. Using my ability to 'read' a person based on their clothing, then change their life by changing their clothes, is a dream come true.

THE CHALLENGES

Undressed came out immediately after my mother, Sylvia, passed away after a battle with a rare neurological condition called MSA-C. Three days after she passed, I had to shoot promotional photos on set. It was challenging because I knew she would want me to keep going as this show was a shared dream, but I had to suspend my grieving. Mum would always say that her happiest moments were when we were together: editing my books, brainstorming ideas, or wearing and helping me sell socks at my first trade shows.

I feel so blessed to have had a mother who encouraged my creativity and who didn't suffocate my dreams with a desire to 'keep me safe'. She was my great collaborator, so I was moved to tears when my team suggested we dedicate the series to her.

ADVICE

Ask yourself what unique talents and passions you can bring to the industry and believe in those gifts even when the world can't recognise them yet. Study the greats, be it designers, photographers, models, editors, directors, producers, writers, fashion historians and editors, and the business aspect. The more you deeply understand your field, the more likely you will be able to contribute at the highest level.

NEGIN MIRSALEHI

INFLUENCER, BEAUTY ENTREPRENEUR, CREATOR OF HAIR CARE BRAND GISOU

Negin Mirsalehi is a fashion and beauty blogger boasting a social media following of more than four million people. She is the creator of the hair care brand GISOU, which is made from pure honey inspired by her father's bee garden and her love of bees.

Growing up, I never specifically knew what I wanted to do as a job, and this was still an issue for me until I graduated from University. My journey as an online influencer started three to four years ago, when I was still a full-time student at the University of Amsterdam. I was writing my thesis when a friend of mine recommended to start with Instagram. It was on Instagram that I became familiar with various bloggers and became curious about what the blogging phenomena really entailed. After some research and seeing what it was all about, I realised that this was something that was made for me. I did not start like most bloggers did 10 years ago who started posting pictures, which turned into being their full-time job. The journey I had was more planned; becoming a big worldwide blogger and making it my career was really one of my purposes. But I did not expect my blog and Instagram to blow up so fast into something so big.

When I started my own website a few years ago, I would only post blogs about my personal fashion taste. Because social media has become so popular, I only use those platforms now to do that. My website's purpose is to inspire my followers with stories. When I started on Instagram my main goal was to inspire, pretty much the same as it is now. But back then, I was still studying, so I had to combine both. After my study I was so happy that I could completely focus on my passion. I really feel that focus is very important when it comes to chasing your dreams.

BUILDING A FOLLOWING

My followers started to increase quite rapidly. I always aimed for collaborations with brands such as Louis Vuitton, Dolce & Gabbana, Dior and more. To achieve this, you have to put yourself on the map. Who are you, and what do you do? Do you take your job seriously? Is there a connection? It took some time to get there, but I am very proud of all the collaborations I have done so far.

In the beginning, I only shared my outfits of the day on Instagram. At a certain point, I realised I wanted to share more of what I do, so I started to post more personal things like my beauty routine and the food I ate, but also stuff pertaining to my education, my family and our love for bees. Since I decided to do that, I've noticed that I've attracted more people and that my interaction has greatly increased. I guess that's the result of people feeling as though they know me better on a more personal and intimate level. It's clear that the more personal things you share, the more people will connect to you and like it. That's why YouTubers who make vlogs have huge followings. For me, I only share the things I feel comfortable with. I will never share everything.

CREATING A BRAND

Before I decided to start my Instagram account, I had created a clear vision and plan for my account; this helped me a lot. From day one, I knew I wanted to focus on creating high-quality content with a cosmopolitan character. The story began with my father, who is a beekeeper, and my mother, who is a hairdresser. Some of my fondest childhood memories stem from growing up in the bee garden. It was my playground and a place filled with only positive vibes, laughter and lots of love.

THE EVOLUTION OF GISOU

Gisou has been born naturally out of my passion for bees, the bee garden and beauty. You could say beekeeping has always been in my blood. My father learnt it from his father, who was taught by my great-grandfather and so on. When moving to the Netherlands, my mother started experimenting with her own hair care solutions. One thing my mother knew for sure was that my dad's honey was going to be the key ingredient. Now, I got the opportunity to combine my love for family and beauty into the brand Gisou.

Four years ago, when I started on Instagram with inspirational fashion posts, I acknowledged that a lot of people were interested in my hair. After receiving so many questions about my hair, I felt like I had something to offer, and I decided to share the healing powers of bee products. This resulted in Gisou, a bee-based hair product line. I knew that the story was of a special nature. However, I never thought that people would be interested in bees or the bee story behind the brand. I definitely believe that people can resonate with the story as it is very authentic and real. I try to share my personal story via my Instagram account and YouTube channel, where my followers can see me work in my father's bee garden or my moments with my mom when she is doing my hair.

THE FUTURE

We are currently working very hard on more hair care products for Gisou. I am so proud to be able to expand this line, as it is something that is so dear to me. It includes my family and my most cherished childhood memories in the Mirsalehi bee garden. We are currently busy with expanding our Gisou hair product line, so exciting things are happening!

We have launched two hair products, both containing ingredients produced by honeybees. The Gisou Honey Infused Hair Oil is an exclusive hair oil enriched with honey from my dad's bee garden. With help from my mum, we were able to use the healing power of honey to create a multi-purpose hair oil. The Gisou Propolis Heat Protecting Spray protects hair from damage caused by the heat of blow dryers, styling tools and the sun. We are working hard on new products and formulas, so stay tuned for some new Gisou!

THE IMPORTANCE OF SOCIAL MEDIA

I have a very solid follower base, which makes them potential Gisou customers. My followers trust me in some sort of way and consider me an influencer. They were open to trying my product because of their interest in my hair. Even though they trust both me and Gisou, the products we offer have to be of good quality in order for them to become a loyal customer. I believe that quality is the key ingredient of Gisou, as I always try to find the best formulas; for example, the formulas that my mother created for the Honey Infused Hair Oil that work so extremely well.

Whether it is about Gisou or the collaborations that I take on with brands, I always take time to think about my ideas and the proper way to execute them.

The beauty industry is very diverse, and I believe that what makes Gisou so special is not only that I launched a bee-based hair care line which delivers quality but also the story of the Mirsalehi bees and my personal story.

When I started my Instagram account, I worked day and night to make it into something that would inspire others. Currently, I am always thinking of new ideas to keep inspiring my followers. When I created my brand, Gisou, it was of great importance that we made sure that the brand would also stand out on social media and inspire women to take care of their hair. I believe that healthy hair is beautiful hair, and with Gisou, I want to share this message. In this day and age, it is important to adapt your marketing strategy to your target group. Thus, social media is definitely a key aspect of our strategy. We see that satisfied customers share their purchases online and we continuously get tagged in pictures of happy customers on the Gisou Instagram page @gisou_official. This makes it very real for us, having the customers share their experience online and would like to be associated with Gisou. I also like to share images of loyal customers through my social media channels.

THE IMPORTANCE OF PASSION

I believe that success starts with passion, I was lucky enough to have found my passion during my study in Business Administration and Marketing. But without perseverance and dedication, I would

have never been where I am at the moment. Strive for your goals no matter what and surround yourself with people who support you in this. Thereby, planning and market research can be of essence before you start something.

My recipe for success is to work very hard and never forget the reason why it started, which to me is my passion for fashion, beauty and lifestyle. Also, it helps a lot to surround myself with positive people who get our work spirit. I also feel very lucky to have my boyfriend as my business partner because we have the same goals, and he's the best when it comes to handling the business side. Lastly, I really feel that focus is very important when it comes to chasing your dreams.

NEGIN'S TIPS

- *My most important advice is to do research and see how you can do things differently. Nowadays, I feel like a lot of girls create mind-blowing content. But only with that, chances are high that you won't be able to turn your passion into your profession.*

- *Try to see what it takes to make that work: think about your reach and how different social platforms can benefit that.*

- *Also, always keep your eyes open for new platforms.*

IRENE KRAUZE

FOUNDER OF BEQUARTII

Irene Krauze is a fashion designer based in Paris with a unique style. She has created a much-loved fashion brand that has been featured on covers of Vogue *and is worn throughout Paris and world-wide.*

STARTING IN THE FASHION INDUSTRY
I came into the fashion industry from architecture. I had a desire to transfer my love for minimalism in architecture to clothes. From that moment on, I started sketching, and this is how the first collection was created.

CREATING THE BRAND
After creating my own brand, 80% of my wardrobe is from Bequartii. Sometimes I buy new clothes from other brands; these are usually basic items that can be worn year after year.

I like to play with masculine and feminine codes. My style has become more minimalistic over the years.

My brand is very important to me. I work a lot, from starting with the sketching and ending with the finished product. I believe clothing does act as a means of communication and as an instrument of influence on the behaviour and attitude of other people.

PASSION FOR STYLE AND FASHION
In my childhood, my grandmother loved to create beautiful handmade clothes for me. She influenced my worldview and gave rise to my individuality. Fashion has always been a part of my life, although I realised this later.

YOUR FIRST BIG BREAK
When Bequartii 's dress was chosen for the cover of *Vogue* magazine. And further orders from customers came from all over the world.

CHALLENGES
A few months after our opening, the pandemic began, and the administration banned showrooms in Paris. It was very tough for our new brand.

We were starting to develop our atelier and were lucky that many of our clients began to order tailor-made clothes from our collections.

ADVICE FOR WOMEN
Let your passions lead you. I think not trying is worse than failing. So don't be afraid of failing. Never compare yourself with anyone. Just work on yourself and become the best version of yourself.

Don't wear clothes in colours that don't match your skin tone. Get to know your silhouette.

ADVICE ON PUTTING A GREAT OUTFIT TOGETHER
Don't rule anything out until you've tried it on to see if it works. Only awareness of your own attractiveness is able to bring a fashion look to the absolute.

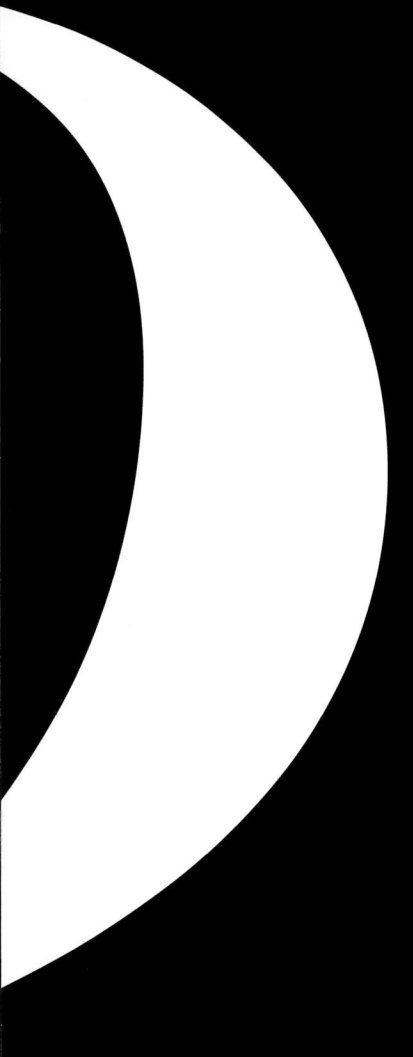

PEOPLE RESPOND WELL TO PEOPLE WHO ARE SURE OF WHAT THEY WANT.

ANNA WINTOUR

SAMANTHA BRETT

BESTSELLING AUTHOR, FOUNDER OF NAKED SUNDAYS

A former national TV news reporter and anchor in Australia, Samantha Brett is the Founder and CEO of the Australian brand Naked Sundays, an SPF product range with world-first multitasking skincare-makeup benefits for the face and body.

I had been a news reporter for *Sunrise* for almost a decade, and I was out in the blazing sun for hours on end with a full face of makeup. I started to notice a rise in melanomas in my colleagues and circle of friends and got to thinking about my own use of sunscreen (or lack of!). Working on the number 1 breakfast show in Australia, you do your makeup at around 3.30am, so even if I did remember to put on sunscreen at that time, it had well and truly worn off by the time the sun came up.

Plus, according to the TGA (Therapeutic Goods Administration Australia), sunscreen needs to be topped up every two hours. I got to thinking about how I could top up my sunscreen throughout the day while at work. And I quickly realised there was a huge gap in the market for sunscreen that wasn't white or sticky, and that would work well OVER makeup. There was no such thing in Australia!

I got to working on a sunscreen that could be sprayed over makeup that was also high-performance SPF and good for your skin. Manufacturers told me it couldn't be done, but I kept going.

Eventually I came up with the now award-winning SPF50+ Hydrating Glow Mist. After we launched Naked Sundays in January 2021, the product instantly sold out in three weeks. People were saying it was the product they'd been searching for and desperately needed.

After doing research into the use of SPF and the generation most at risk of melanoma, I realised it was 16-35-year-olds who had the highest rate of melanoma. So I thought that if I could get the younger generation using and loving SPF from an early age, we could start to change the habits early, and hopefully improve the high rate of melanoma.

It's definitely a journey and one that has me working 24/7, 365 days a year. If there were more hours in the day, you'd find me working them!

After we launched initially and saw the success right away after filling a huge gap in the market for SPF50+ designed to be worn OVER makeup, we knew we were on to something. We were lucky enough to exclusively partner with Mecca (Australia's number 1 beauty retailer) early on to launch our brand more widely across Australia. When we did launch into the Mecca stores in October 2021, it was towards the end of lockdowns, and people were so eager to get back into the stores. We ended up selling out of our two hero SKUs in 24 hours! We experienced a 400% in the first year, but we are still a very small and hardworking team.

Naked Sundays is 100% focused on high-performance SPF50% that is easy to use and can be reapplied over makeup or worn on its own. All our products double up and multi-task as skincare, so you only need one product in the morning. We also have world-first formulas, such as our world-first lip oil with SPF50 and our world-first Clear SPF Serum with SPF50. We focus on education and aim to change the habits of the younger generation so they don't end up where my generation is today, and we do that by providing super-fun, cool, high-performance products that are easy to use and fit seamlessly into any beauty routine.

I spent two years with Steph interviewing women for *The Game Changers*. Throughout the book, incredible entrepreneurs shared their stories and that inspired to execute any idea I had without any fear. The biggest lesson most of the women had in common was feeling the fear and doing it anyway. And funnily enough, that's what encouraged me to start Naked Sundays.

There are so many exciting things in the pipeline for Naked Sundays, but the main focus is changing the habits of one sunscreen-hating person at a time.

SAM'S TIPS

- *Know that running a business is NOT glamorous like it might seem on socials. There is a myriad of moving parts that you won't even know existed, and it's important as an entrepreneur that you learn and know how to run every facet of your business, from freight to formulations, to legal, to website design – I've learnt it all!*

- *Read, read, read. Not just about people in your chosen field of work but everything. The news, self-help books, inspirational stories – anything that will get your creative juices flowing.*

- *Wear your sunscreen every single day!*

- *Be the hardest-working person in the room.*

ALEXANDRA MCGUIGAN

FOUNDER & CEO, INCLUSIVE ASSET MANAGEMENT

After 10 years working in Finance and being dubbed 'The Billion Dollar Girl', Alexandra McGuigan set up Inclusive Asset Management to tackle the under-representation of women in asset management. She has received global recognition for her work in the Diversity Equity & Inclusion space, primarily for her advocacy for women in investment management.

I always loved school. I clearly remember showing up for the first day at kindergarten and children were crying. I couldn't understand it. I had been desperate to go ever since my older sister had started two years prior.

My favourite subject was maths but when I started high school, I was put into an advanced class and didn't do well. That experience led me on a different path, and I studied Arts at university.

Much to my father's dismay I decided to pursue acting, which is an extremely tough career. When that didn't work out, he encouraged me to do an MBA to see what else was out there. After all those years, I found my way back to the study of finance and economics and realised that not only was I good at it, but I loved it.

I am now an entrepreneur, speaker, Board Director, and Gender Diversity campaigner, and I've worked with some of the biggest names in Asset Management.

BUILDING MY CAREER

I decided that I wanted to spend part of my studies in France, to have an adventure and learn another language.

To get to Paris though, I was going to need some money. Encouraged by my renewed interest in study, I applied for a few different positions and was ready to work my way up the corporate ladder.

In early 2007, I was hired by the CEO of BNY Mellon Asset Management for an entry level position. The business was just starting in Australia, so everyone had to get their hands dirty and really work on everything. After a short time, I knew I was on the right path and that I wanted to work in Financial Services. I tried to be like a sponge and learn everything that I could about the asset

management industry. This experience changed the trajectory of my career.

QUALITIES FOR SUCCESS
I believe you need to have resilience and courage, and to be kind (to others, but also to yourself).

GOALS AND PURPOSE
Women are not only under-represented in numbers in the industry, but also in the amount of money that they manage. My goal is simple: to have more money managed by female investors. I work with both female fund managers and institutional investors to do this.

INSPIRATION
My mother has always been my source of inspiration. She was a trailblazer as the first female radiation oncologist in NSW, Australia in the late 1970s. At the time there was a similar under-representation of women in medicine as remains today in finance.

DEFINING MOMENT
When I got my first big job, I set a goal to raise $1 billion. People thought I was crazy, but I didn't really care. I worked tirelessly, constantly on the road, sometimes doing 30-40 meetings in a week and then flying back home, only to do it all again. I absolutely loved the adrenalin, though, and within two years, I had achieved my goal, and then some! When I visited the fund manager's office, they introduced me as 'the Billion Dollar Girl' and the name stuck.

FUTURE ASPIRATIONS
To launch my own fund that enables big investors to find and allocate to talented female fund managers easily.

ALEXANDRA'S TIPS

- *Study Maths and Finance. It will give you options.*

- *Just start investing, no matter how small. There is nothing like real-life experience to draw from in an interview.*

- *Set a goal. A clear direction sets the compass and helps to guide the path.*

- *Don't be shy, take your place. There has never been a better place for women in finance.*

- *Always reach for the stars. I always talk about the power of visualisation. Visualise what you want, and don't give up until you get it!*

VIIVI AVELLAN

CO-FOUNDER OF VIILEE SOLUTIONS LLC

A trailblazer, Viivi Avellan has worked as a sports news reporter and news anchor to a producer at Finland's national TV channel and has also served as the editor-in-chief of the premier Finnish golf magazine.

In my childhood years, my interests included sports, politics, and making self-made news video clips with my small personal video camera. At school, I loved arts, all kinds of sports and social sciences. I embraced a diverse range of activities, from cheerleading on the school's team to actively engaging in the IT club. After school, I knew I couldn't be confined to a single box but, rather, I decided to venture out of my comfort zone to find adventures.

BUILDING MY CAREER

My career hasn't really followed a straight path, but the experience that altered everything was golf.

Competing at the national level, I developed an intense passion for the game – I literally lived and breathed golf back then. Ironically, during my early years, my parents insisted that my brother and I engage in golf, piano, and skiing and of those three, golf was my least favourite pastime. The thought of attending golf lessons felt burdensome because I felt that to learn something, you needed to really get in there on the course and not just practise on the driving range. Yet, to my surprise, my attitude shifted, and I gradually directed my focus and attention towards actually studying and learning about golf.

Thanks to golf, or rather my deep understanding of the sport, I received my first permanent job offer with a nationwide TV channel's production team. Initially tasked with drafting inserts for a programme centred around golf, I swiftly received training from the media corporation to transition into the role of a sports news reporter. Within a mere two months, I found myself anchoring live news broadcasts. For the remainder of my career in the media industry, I served as both a news anchor and a producer.

A TURNING POINT TOWARD SUCCESS

My time as a news reporter gave me the incredible opportunity to not only explore new avenues but also gain significant exposure in the media. This undoubtedly played a pivotal role in propelling my career to the next stages.

One of the most significant turning points in my career was resigning from my position as a news reporter after eight years, due to the enormous publicity the job brought with it. It was a decision that drove me into uncharted territory, but I believed that new opportunities would arise, and I really needed a break from hectic work and publicity. This is when I started writing my first book, *The Bachelorette's Bible*. To my complete surprise, a little over a year later, I was in Switzerland, where I hosted an art gallery for three years.

CAREER CHALLENGES

My early career in news production laid a solid foundation for my ability to work and perform under pressure. The fast-paced environment of news production demands efficiency every minute, resulting in the intense pressure of live news broadcasts. I had to be alert and sharp every single day.

Over time, I grew accustomed to the demands of the job. I became less susceptible to stress over minor issues, and my resilience in high-pressure situations improved significantly. It wasn't until later, in very different work environments, that I noticed

my colleagues were struggling to cope with hectic situations while I actually enjoyed it.

Now, as I assist European entrepreneurs in their expansion efforts into new territories, I recognise that one of the biggest challenges is helping them understand the huge cultural differences between different countries and the great risks they face if they do not grasp the target country's culture, rules of society and legal regulations The pandemic presented immense challenges for me, both in my professional endeavours and on a personal level. Just six months after I invested in a very prominent gym company in Finland, it went bankrupt due to the pandemic's economic strain. Similarly, I was compelled to sell my wellness company in Singapore for a considerably lower price than I had initially anticipated. Moreover, the loss of my mother to cancer during the pandemic really pushed me into a very dark place mentally for a while.

Thankfully, the unwavering support of my husband and children kept me afoot during this very dark period in my life. Despite my resolve to refrain from setting up another company, the entrepreneurial spirit within me was alive. A year later, I found myself embarking on a new business venture in California.

IMPACT

I feel that one of my missions is to help empower women. I encourage women to establish their own companies and help existing successful businesses expand into the U.S. I've motivated many women to embrace entrepreneurship and admire their success. I aspire to have a lasting career in encouraging, advising, and serving entrepreneurs.

VIIVI'S TIPS

- *Dare to leap into the unknown, because without taking that leap, you cannot fly.*

- *Envision the bigger picture.*

- *Establish personal goals.*

- *Have a strong belief in your vision.*

- *Refuse to yield to adversities if immediate success is not there.*

GAY GASSMANN

CONTRIBUTING EDITOR OF ARCHITECTURAL DIGEST USA, VOGUE ARABIA, VOGUE ARABIA LIVING AND AD CHINA

CAREER CHALLENGES
One of the biggest challenges, which will be no secret to most women, is the fear of not being up to what you think other people think about you.

From my experience, I had to pivot from the insecurity of being the only Asian woman in the room to taking all of this as an accomplishment and propelling me further. Because of this, I think my most important lesson was to learn to trust myself and take things from there.

WORKING IN THE FASHION INDUSTRY
The thrill of attending a live fashion show never gets old. The early days, when I first arrived in Paris as a student, standing up at the back at YSL with all of those white flowers, drama and music, hooked me for life! It was always a special treat to attend the YSL shows, and the last show, at the Centre Georges Pompidou, had me in tears. I know that sounds cliché, but that's the truth.

Fast forward to today, and to attend any Chanel show takes my breath away.

I also make a point of attending and supporting friends like Alexis Mabille but also seeking out the younger emerging designers, perhaps showing for the first time. I pay attention to what I call around the edges. Not the big brands who have amazing budgets and shows, but perhaps the younger kid, showing in a parking lot somewhere or in a garage.

I'm keeping my eye on them.

PERSONAL STYLE
I think if I were to describe my personal style now, which in fact doesn't seem to have changed over the years... Classic chic, with a touch of fun, easy to wear and always a big mix and match. I love the comfort of Chanel but always with something a bit off, in unexpected colours and bold jewellery. Real, costume collector, but always big and with meaning to me personally.

DIGITAL LANDSCAPE
The digital landscape is super-exciting, and I'm following what the kids are doing very closely.

It's definitely part of the future, but again, for me, it's not one or the other. I actually recently joined the advisory board for a community-driven creative studio with a focus on art, music and fashion-funded NFTS @heartnfts. I'm running to keep up with great interest and excitement.

ADVICE

I know this sounds cliché, but always be yourself. There is nothing more attractive than someone who knows who they are and embraces whatever that may be. The days of wanting to look like this or that person have evolved.

PERSONAL STYLE

Certain things convey in one way or another, different messages. I think people are always intrigued and curious about the person who seems to just throw things on and step out the door with confidence, kindness and a great smile.

I guess what needs to be said is that the way we dress, our personal style, speaks volumes about who we are, where we are going, but also, how we feel about where we are. In an old-fashioned kind of way, I like to put my best foot forward and dress thinking about who I will be with and what my style is saying about me. I always appreciate someone who takes care of their appearance, but not in any fussy kind of way, and also, the style has nothing to do with the budget.

INSPIRATION

I am always happy to see people who have found their place in the fashion world by being themselves, regardless of what's trendy or hot at any given moment. I respect Vanessa Friedman for her laser-sharp eye, brilliant writing and honest point of view about the fashion world. I also always have an eye on what the young creatives are doing and how they are navigating the rapidly changing landscape of what it means to be in fashion and the fashion world. For this, my secret weapon is my daughter, Amalie Gassman, who has grown up in the fashion and art worlds, worked professionally as a model since she was sixteen and is currently launching an NFT project.

GAY'S TIPS

- *Always be yourself.*

- *Embrace your career path, whatever that may be.*

- *Trust in who you are.*

> *WE HAVE TO RESHAPE OUR OWN PERCEPTION OF HOW WE VIEW OURSELVES. WE HAVE TO STEP UP AS WOMEN AND TAKE THE LEAD.*
>
> **BEYONCÉ**

NOELLA COURSARIS MUSUNKA

FOUNDER OF MALAIKA

Noella Musunka's Malaika is a non-profit that operates in the Democratic Republic of Congo. It aims to empower the next generation of changemakers through access to education, sport and health programs for girls and their communities.

I had quite a difficult childhood, with my dad passing when I was five. My mother knew I wouldn't get an education if I stayed in Congo as she didn't have the financial means to support it. I was an only child, so she sent me to live in Europe with some family. I still had hopes and dreams for my future, and so I felt I had two choices: feel disheartened by the difficult circumstances I found myself in and give up, or recognise that if I worked hard and gained an education, I could still achieve my dreams.

In terms of a vocation, I wanted to be a doctor. I think I've always wanted to work with people, and I loved the thought of being someone who helped others. I'm so grateful that my career has afforded me the platform from which I can impact others for the better.

STARTING OUT

My friends advised me to enter a competition with Agent Provocateur, and I was selected. I did their campaign, and from there, I went on to do other modelling work in both New York and London, appearing in publications such as *Vogue*, *Marie Claire*, *Vanity Fair* and *ELLE*. My career really took off after the Agent Provocateur campaign. I started to get more consistent work and increasingly high-profile campaigns as well. I think that's often the case; you get your one break that changes things and propels you forward. You just have to dig in, keep working, stay positive and not give up before that happens.

GIVING BACK

I set up Malaika in 2007 after realising the immense opportunity I had to make a difference by using the voice I now had through my modelling career. Malaika is based in the Democratic Republic of Congo and is a free, accredited school that provides a holistic primary and secondary education to 346 girls, ranging from STEM (Science, Technology, Engineering, Maths) and coding to art, music, theatre and sport. Malaika also has a community centre that was built in partnership with FIFA. It offers a range of programmes to 5000 youth and adults in the wider community.

What makes the Malaika model special is that we have empowered the entire community with education and health programs, not just the children. Our staff and volunteers on the ground are Congolese, and many parents of the students have benefited from being able to contribute to the upkeep of the centre and school. We have a plantation that enables adults and youths to gain entrepreneurial skills as well as provide food for the students. We have built and refurbished 19 wells so that 30,000 people in the local area can access clean water, as well as improving the general infrastructure of the village.

Nothing is wasted at Malaika. We use every physical need of the people and the facilities as an opportunity to teach, develop and empower children and adults to live healthier and more productive lives. Malaika's community-driven approach acts as a model that can be replicated on a global scale in communities across the world. We are currently working on putting it all down in an accessible format for others to follow.

I am overwhelmed when I think of the first days of one classroom, a handful of students, and many, many barriers to learning which were hindering the girls who came to school. Now, 346 students walk through the doors of our incredible facility. They come from sleeping on the floor to a building where they use toilets, eat with cutlery and operate IT equipment. When I see the five-year-olds who first join the school and how they are enabled to express themselves and then the older students who are now writing HTML webpages – it's unbelievable to me. They have so much potential.

What Malaika is today is the result of a team of staff and volunteers who have worked incredibly hard; some internationally and others on the ground in Congo, working to help embed Malaika and encourage the community to value the education of its girls and support them in attending school. The journey has involved us continually listening to our beneficiaries and trying to meet the challenges they face. For example, the issue of a lack of clean water was significant. It increased the spread of waterborne diseases and took up a lot of the girls' time as they had to travel long distances to fetch water for their families, preventing them from accessing education. When we started building wells, it had a big impact, and we have just kept working to grow what we have in every area. Years after that first well was built we have 19 wells serving 30,000 people.

THE CHALLENGES

Congo is a challenging country to work in. At the start, it was difficult to set up the foundation due to the instability the country was facing at the time. Fundraising is a consistent challenge. It has been important to me from the start to ensure that money donated to Malaika funds the programmes and doesn't get absorbed by a lot of overheads. Eighty-five per cent of what we raise goes into the programmes. It is challenging to raise the money required for the upkeep of the facilities and all the programmes we run without a large workforce. I am so grateful for the many volunteers we have who help sustain us.

MY BIGGEST SUCCESS

My biggest success will always be my two children, JJ and Cara. It fills me with pride every day to be their mother, and that will always be an important part of my identity. I also see it as a success to be healthy, especially in this day and age when there are a lot of demands on our time, and it can be easy to not make maintaining both our mental and physical health a priority. Of course, a big success for me was the day we opened Malaika. The memory of seeing the girls arrive at school on their first stay will always stay with me as one of my proudest moments.

THE SIDE HUSTLE

I think it's important for women to be creative and to give to others. If you can't be especially creative in your work, then having a side hustle that allows you to express yourself is great. I also believe it is important for every person to do things that have meaning and that bring meaning to others. So, I'd encourage any woman to see how their work, side hustle, or hobby could benefit others and improve the lives of people less fortunate.

SOCIAL MEDIA

Social media is word of mouth multiplied by millions! It has raised the profile of Malaika and enabled young people to reach out to us and support us by volunteering and fundraising. Most good things have a downside, and in order for social media to be a force for good, we do have to manage how we use it. I would say keep being true to yourself, and it's important to keep your distance from it sometimes.

MY ROLE MODELS

Nelson Mandela and Rosa Parks have been key aspirational figures for me who have fought for what they believe in at great personal cost. Rosa Parks made a stand for equal rights in what may have felt like a small way to her, but she ended up triggering one of the biggest social movements in history. As well as these famous men and women, a source of inspiration for me is women all over the world who live and raise families in rural conditions.

I learn so much from them. Their perseverance and determination to continually mould a better future for themselves have impacted me significantly throughout my life.

NOELLA'S MOTTO

I've always had the motto "Model with Meaning" when it comes to my work. Whilst that still applies, I would say my motto has developed to be "do everything with meaning". Keep looking for how you can use your talents, skills, education, and success to benefit the world and its people.

NOELLA'S TIPS

- *Never give up.*

- *Get a great team of like-minded, passionate people around you.*

- *Stay positive, and keep believing that every problem has a solution.*

LAURIE ADAMS

PRESIDENT OF WOMEN FOR WOMEN INTERNATIONAL

Laurie Adams is a true champion of women, dedicating her life to helping others. She is the President of Women For Women International, which focuses on empowering female survivors of war. The organisation has served almost half a million women who have survived wars in Afghanistan, Bosnia-Herzegovina, the Democratic Republic of the Congo, Iraq, Kosovo, Nigeria, Rwanda and South Sudan.

My personal and professional life has been a global one. I was born in Korea and raised in Europe. I went to school in the United States and started working in South Africa while still in college. I was the chair of the founding board of The Other Foundation, which focuses on equality and freedom in southern Africa, with a focus on sexual orientation and gender identity. I also served as a director on the boards of The Forum for the Empowerment of Women in South Africa and ActionAid Brazil and for eight years at ActionAid International. Before joining Women for Women International, I was the Director of Women's Rights for Oxfam in the United Kingdom and managed three country programmes in African regions.

My university degree was in Government with a Minor in Education and a certificate in Gender Studies, but my real learning took place outside the classroom. I was very active in student movements to end racism and sexism on campus – including to get Dartmouth to divest from the apartheid government in South Africa. I learned how to negotiate with power holders such as trustees and the administration, how to speak publicly and how to write and edit and make my voice heard. I also learned desktop publishing, fundraising and organising while working on campus and in South Africa to end apartheid and advance equality.

CHANGING SOUTH AFRICA
Growing up with a black sister, I witnessed racism in a personal way. It made me see that racism isn't an issue that impacted nameless strangers, but one that impacted my own family. This led me to join the anti-apartheid movement and devote my life to it. When Mandela was released in 1990, I was given the incredible opportunity to move there and represent two US organizations. I leaped at the chance to help build a new democratic South Africa and the decision changed my life.

I did a wide range of work in South Africa. I started out working with US organisations and then had the opportunity to work with local institutions. Later, I was able to work in global organisations, and I had the chance to live, visit, and work in more than 20 African countries. I have had the great privilege of spending months amongst nomadic people in places like Kenya and Mali discussing gender roles, being at the bargaining table with ministers and even presidents deciding trade rules and being a first responder, saving lives from conflict and natural disasters ranging from Liberia to Angola. South Africa was a fantastic start to a life full of adventure, growth and learning for me.

WOMEN FOR WOMEN INTERNATIONAL
Women for Women International (WfWI) is a grassroots organisation committed to long-term and sustainable investment in the empowerment of women survivors of war around the world. We work with the most marginalised and socially-excluded women so they have the skills, networks, and tools they need to rebuild their lives, communities, and nations. Through our comprehensive 12-month programme, women learn about their rights and health and gain key life, vocational, and business skills to access livelihoods and break free from trauma and poverty. We have served more than 462,000 women survivors of war in Afghanistan, Bosnia-Herzegovina, the Democratic Republic of the Congo, Iraq, Kosovo, Nigeria, Rwanda and South Sudan.

What I love about Women for Women International's work is its comprehensive nature. We don't work only on economic empowerment, or only on health – we work with women as whole human beings with many facets in their lives. Our programme helps women become economically empowered, but we also provide information about health and well-being and family planning. We also make it possible for women to create savings groups and support systems and teach women about their rights and the value of their lives and their work. In addition, we work with men. Through our work, we've learned that when men are not engaged as allies in the fight for equality in their communities, they bring in more men and create a ripple effect of change. This is why we ensure that the men we work with know about women's rights and the value of women's lives and work as well. We've reached more than 15,000 men through our men's engagement programme.

EXPANDING THE REACH
During a recent trip to Nigeria, the Women for Women International staff noticed that on enrolment day for our programme, hundreds of women were standing at a church parking lot to sign up. The programme had reached its limit for new enrolments, and the women were told that the classes were full and they should go home. They didn't. Rather, they came back the next day, and the day after, and the day after that, hoping a spot would open for them. At WfWI, we are always thinking about how we can expand our work. We want to reach women where they are. Right now, we are opening a country office in Erbil in Northern Iraq and exploring opening an office in Jordan to serve more Syrian and Iraqi refugees. We are also finding partners to work with in South Sudan, where famine and unrest are threatening the lives of many and have displaced 3.5 million people.

As we look to the future, we are aiming for a day when we will not have to turn away another woman, when we will have the capacity to accept every single woman in that church parking lot.

SUPPORTING WOMEN AFFECTED BY ISIS
We see time and time again that during modern conflicts, women's bodies are used as battlefields, and rape is a weapon to silence and marginalise women. In Iraq and Syria, ISIS has abducted thousands of women, sold them in marketplaces like commodities, and turned them into sexual slaves. Even after escaping or being freed from ISIS, women live with an immense amount of trauma; the fabrics of their communities and families are broken, and they are left without any support systems. In addition to the overt physical violence against and sexual exploitation of women committed by ISIS, millions of women and their families have been displaced or become refugees due to the conflict.

Women continue to face violence and abuse as they flee, on the way, and in many refugee camps. After being uprooted from their communities and sometimes losing the male head of household to conflict, women need to find new livelihoods to sustain their families in addition to dealing with trauma. The needs are immense, and we are trying to fill some of that gap. Through partnerships with

local organisations, WfWI provides women with life and vocational skills, training, psychosocial therapy, and classes on rights and health. Our work is focused on providing women not only with healing but also with opportunities to thrive, earn an income, rebuild lives, and ensure better futures.

Our work in the region started in 2015. Recently, with support from the UN Trust Fund to End Violence against Women (UNTF), we have been able to increase the number of women we serve in the region. Over the next three years, we will provide psychosocial support services and life and business skills training to 3000 Syrian and Yezidi women to help them overcome trauma and empower themselves. Through local partners, we are working to reach the most vulnerable women in need of support, including those suffering severe emotional trauma, at high risk of violence, and living in extreme poverty.

WOMEN SUPPORTING WOMEN

I always believed I must use the gifts and privileges I was given to help others – especially those experiencing extreme injustice. It was over the years of working on a wide range of issues, such as racism, poverty, and economic and social inequality, that I saw how deeply gender equality cuts across all of those. Whether you are in a peaceful country or a war-torn one, a rich country or an impoverished one, gendered discrimination and inequality are present across all communities in different degrees. It is unacceptable that one out of three women on earth have faced physical or sexual violence, that every year, 15 million girls are married before their 18th birthday, and that many still call this a 'cultural issue' or a 'domestic decision'. This is a human rights issue and it impacts every one of us.

Secretary Hillary Clinton is definitely a champion of women. She was the featured speaker at our luncheon in 2017. She spoke to a room of more than 500 guests and urged them to support the work that we do. She lent us her voice and said, "During the course of my years of working on behalf of these issues, this organisation (WfWI) is one that has really produced results." She also said that "women's rights are the unfinished business of the 21st century," and we agree that there is a lot of work to be done, and there are many ways to get it done. I deeply believe that the work that WfWI does is unique and extremely efficient in finishing this business. Our numbers show it, too. When a woman joins our programme, her daily income is $0.34. When she graduates, it triples to $1.07. While before joining our programme, 30% of women used family planning; after the programme, 87% reported using it. Before our programme, 10% of the women we work with say they talk to other women about their rights. After our programme, 89% say they do so. And one of the most fantastic and most empowering parts of our work is that anyone can contribute.

BEING A POWERHOUSE

Being a Powerhouse is able to bring people together to act around a vision – that takes listening deeply, charting the collective path, then keeping that arm on the tiller/rudder quite firmly: ready to both hold and change course.

LAURIE'S TIPS

- *Believe in yourself (while constantly striving to improve).*

- *Believe in your vision.*

- *Challenge your own thinking and inform your decisions with data and with people who disagree with you.*

- *Embrace error or "fail forward fast": Don't worry about mistakes. Learn from them (and don't make the same one again).*

- *Have fun! The journey to change is a long one. You have to sustain yourself!*

MELISSA ODABASH

FASHION DESIGNER

A former swimwear model, Melissa Odabash launched her eponymous swimwear collection in 1999. The collection swiftly came to epitomise the glamour and sophistication of a luxury lifestyle brand and was named by British Vogue as "The Ferrari of the bikini world". Her label is distributed in over 48 countries and sold in over 250 luxury department stores. It is a favourite line of many A-list stars, including Kate Moss, Gwyneth Paltrow, Beyoncé and the Princess of Wales.

I got into the fashion industry through modelling – I was scouted at a young age and moved to Europe to pursue my modelling career. I was living in Italy and realised that everything I was modelling was too rash or too revealing. The prints and styles were not doing any justice to a woman's body, so I decided to create my own line using high-quality fabrics and simple colours that would suit any woman with any shape.

I wanted to create something that was classic and timeless. I learnt from the swimwear business which fabrics worked and which ones were the better choices for swimwear. I sought out information from buyers to find out what they were looking for when buying swimwear. In addition, I travelled and lived in many countries, so I was able to understand the different markets and demands from customers in these locations. I started out by going from door to door with my samples in Italy, which was tough. Getting paid in Italy was even harder!

BUILDING THE BRAND
A year or so into designing, a friend of mine managed to take some samples of my work over to the United States and managed to get them into *Sports Illustrated* magazine. Seeing my designs on Tyra Banks and Naomi Campbell in the *Sports Illustrated* calendar was an amazing moment for me. Then, two years later, Victoria's Secret stocked one of my designs– a zebra print with a blue border – and this really helped my brand awareness grow!

Over the years, my brand has continued to evolve, and I feel very lucky to have hit many milestones, but I have to say having won several awards in the last couple of years has been such a great time. I won Swimwear Designer of the Year in

London, Designer of the Year in Paris and Retailer of the Year very recently. It's great to be recognised after 15 years of hard work.

THE FUTURE
Next, I will be launching a Ready To Wear Collection, which I am very excited about! I will also be launching more accessories that will complement my core lines.

ADVICE TO WOMEN
Never let anyone tell you that your idea won't work. Stay determined and focus on what your core business is.

Don't worry about failure its part of building a dream. Believe in yourself no matter what someone tells you! Being a boss you don't get a lot of taps on the back.

Be kind to everyone.

EXPANDING THE BRAND
We now are in like fifty-nine countries. I would love to do more franchises so people can have the whole lifestyle of what my brand is about. It's very hard wholesaling as it's just a few bits here and there and you don't get the entire collection. I still believe in stores and shopping – not just online! I'm also launching into more ready to wear. I love working with new fabrics.

WHAT MAKES A POWERHOUSE
Treat everyone equal, never be a 'boss' and treat your team as family – remember, it takes a team to build a company.

MELISSA'S TIPS

- *Never give up focus!*

- *Choose one product and get it right.*

- *Once you have mastered the first product, then look to expand.*

- *Don't do anything just for money; do it for your passion, and money will come later. At least you will love doing what you do!*

> *THERE ARE SECRET OPPORTUNITIES HIDDEN IN EVERY FAILURE.*
>
> SOPHIA AMORUSO

KRISTIN CAVALLARI

FOUNDER AND CEO OF UNCOMMON JAMES, NEW YORK TIMES BESTSELLING AUTHOR

"In business, take the emotion out of your decisions. Don't let a couple of 'no's' discourage you. Keep fighting for what you want!"

I was going to high school in Laguna Beach, California, and out of nowhere, MTV showed up one day and did an open casting. They were doing a reality show about "the real Orange County", and I immediately knew I wanted to be on it. I did an on-camera interview and ended up getting the role. I had no idea what it was going to turn into, and it's been a wild ride ever since!

I felt like I was on top of the world after *Laguna Beach* (I was only 18), and then I was adamant about becoming a serious actress and was quickly back on the bottom. It wasn't until I launched my own company, Uncommon James, that I felt I really found what I was supposed to be doing. The entertainment world is so up and down, so I never really felt secure in that. Uncommon James is my creative outlet, and since I'm the founder and CEO, I have complete creative freedom to do whatever I want, and that's been a dream come true.

After I had acted for a few years and stepped away from reality television, MTV made me an offer to be on *The Hills*. It was a very tough decision because I knew if I went back to reality TV, then my career was going to look very different than I had envisioned at the time. I also made the decision to go back to reality TV when I launched Uncommon James because I knew it would be priceless exposure for the brand, but I was hesitant about letting cameras back in again since I was now a wife and mother.

UNCOMMON JAMES
Uncommon James is my fourth baby. I launched it in the spring of 2017 and it's been a rocket ship ever since, which has been a ton of fun. I wanted a line of jewellery that was easy. I'm designing for the modern woman: she's busy and needs pieces she can throw on with any outfit that can take her from day to night. I just wanted an effortless line that we don't have to overthink. For me, I love having a side hustle. I'm the kind of person that runs on a fast-paced life, that "go, go, go" mentality. I've always needed something to call my own: it's where I get my confidence.

JUGGLING FAMILY
With my family, I stick to a routine and structure, and that really helps. There are certain times (like weekdays at 4pm until bedtime and weekends) that are for family only. The beauty of owning my own business is that I can essentially make my own hours. I'm the one taking my kids to school in the morning and making dinner every night, and that will never change.

THE PRESSURES
Because I've dealt with being in the spotlight for so long, I've gotten a tough skin over the years. But I would be lying if I said it didn't get to me sometimes. My family helps put everything in perspective: none of that noise matters.

As I've gotten older, I've also realised that no matter what we do, we can't please everyone, so we should just live our lives for ourselves.

SOCIAL MEDIA
I have a love/hate relationship with social media! I don't know if Uncommon James would be what it is today without it because, in the early days, that was the only reach we had to our customers. But I also

think it puts a lot of pressure on people today: we are all comparing our worst to everyone else's best, and that's a scary place, especially as a mom.

GIVING BACK
Giving back is something that is extremely important to me. I went to Kenya to rebuild schools and bring children all the supplies they needed, from clean water to clothing and beyond. Now, with Uncommon James, we are partnering with a local organisation called Mother to Mother to bring essentials to families who aren't able to provide for their children. I am also involved in Vital Voices whose mission is to build women leaders.

MY ROLE MODELS
My dad is definitely someone I look up to. He's self-made and has instilled in me that we all create our own destiny. He's always encouraged me to go out there and grab life by the horns. I'm always inspired by other female founders, especially those who are moms. It's tough; it's not for the faint of heart, so I enjoy getting to know some of these women to know we are all going through the same things.

MY TOP BUSINESS ADVICE
My top advice would be to take the emotion out of it and base all decisions solely on what's best for the company. It is also a good idea to get a network of other founders or CEOs (or whatever your role is) to share experiences and help each other out. It's a great support system that's different than what a spouse or friends can give you, and to not let a couple of "no's" discourage you – that's part of life, and you have to keep going and fighting for what you want!

MONIQUE LHUILLIER

FASHION DESIGNER

Established in 1996, Monique Lhuillier has revolutionised the wedding gown industry with her luxurious, feminine label worn by celebrities and fans across the globe. The label is now internationally recognised as one of the world's foremost couture bridal and ready-to-wear brands.

I've always been passionate about design and fashion. I grew up in the Philippines with a very glamorous mother. She loved to entertain, and I would watch her get dressed and help her choose outfits and accessories. My mother had also started a children's clothing business – very tailor-made, special occasion clothes. I learned to choose fabrics, design and fit. Everything about the way I grew up seemed to organically lead me to fashion: the fashion seed was planted early on.

By high school I had already decided I wanted to open my own fashion house and have my own brand with stores around the world. That's what it said in my high school yearbook in 1987! When I graduated I had already determined to study fashion design at FIDM (Fashion Design and Fashion Merchandising in the United States).

When I graduated from FIDM, I was engaged, and the search for a wedding dress proved challenging. In bridal at the time, there were two extreme trends: overly fussy and detailed, or very stark, modern and minimal. I wanted something that was romantic and traditional with a twist, and I saw a niche in the market. Back then, I didn't have a goal; I just wanted to get my business started. I knew that if I was looking for a particular style of wedding dress and I couldn't find it on the market, other women likely felt the same.

While I was planning my wedding, I was working for a small French company designing ready-to-wear. A year after I was married, I found the courage to leave my job and try my hand at starting my own label. I had felt at my own wedding that I had really wanted the experience of being pampered. I wanted to have that experience of being a bride and being looked after and, to be honest, I didn't really get it. When I opened my first boutique, creating that kind of environment and experience was very important to me.

Once multiple orders started coming in, I realised we had begun. For about three years no one knew how to pronounce my name – then one day they could! I felt we'd finally gained a great following and were heading in the right direction.

BUILDING THE BRAND

My husband and I were very young when we got married, and one of the best decisions we made was to wait to start our family so we could focus on building our business. We were young and didn't have much experience. In a sense, we were lucky that one of us had a design background and the other knew how to run a business. We learned from our mistakes, which could sometimes be expensive, which is a challenge for any new business. We worked seven days a week, hosting trunk shows on the weekends.

Our goal at this time was to first make a beautiful product and then build a luxury brand. As soon as we could, we sought to put together a strong team so we could expand with that support. I didn't think at the time that I would grow into a lifestyle brand including home and beauty; I didn't think that far ahead.

At the height of Britney Spears's career, making her Bridal gown created an enormous amount of exposure for my brand. Britney wanted to collaborate on the design and feel of her gown, so I created something I thought expressed her personality as a bride and made her feel that day was special.

Also, Identifying a niche in the market and focusing on a beautiful product were integral to my early success and longevity. Great relationships within the industry have certainly been inherent in our ability to grow. We were determined and committed to the growth of the business.

THE GROWTH

We started with the intention to develop a successful Bridal business, and to open our own retail. My dresses were feminine and traditional, with a modern twist. They were cut very close to the body, which gave them a more youthful energy. Intricate detail with an ethereal lightness was important to me in design and developed as a signature of my Bridal collections. I'm inspired by living, travel, fabric, art, a beautiful piece of embroidery. I like to create a romance and theatre with my designs, so the starting point is often a mood, or a feeling.

I've been fortunate to design for some incredible women for special moments in their lives. I've also enjoyed dressing high-profile women, who throughout my career, have helped take my brand to a larger audience. When I see women in my clothes, it validates what I do.

When we reached a great rhythm in Bridal, we looked at our customer and her life beyond the wedding and thought about how we could grow with her. The next step was launching Evening and Ready To Wear and Diffusion. My fashion categories now also offer Fur, Accessories, Footwear and Eyewear.

After 20 years in business I am proud to have a brand that encompasses fashion and lifestyle. Bridal mainline and two diffusions: engagement rings with Blue Nile. Ready to Wear presents four collections a year and diffusion.

Lifestyle covers Fine Paper to Home Fragrance, fine crystal and collaborations in Home Decor specifically for children and, most recently, my first beauty collaboration. My designs have an incredible representation in retail across the US and internationally – Neiman Marcus has been an amazing partner from the beginning. I'm also proud to have two flagship stores in New York and LA, and would like to open more Monique Lhuillier doors. Neiman Marcus, Bergdorf Goodman, Harrods and Saks Fifth Avenue have also been strong supporters from the very beginning.

THE BABY RANGE

Images had been published of my home, including my children's rooms, so people had seen my space and home design. Pottery Barn Kids reached out for a collaboration because they knew my brand and thought I might be interested in extending my design philosophy into the realm of décor. It was exciting again for me to look at how we grew with this family and how well my aesthetic could translate to children's furniture. Later, with my own children, I had the authority to know what that looked like, and my own experience inspired the collection. As a mother, I knew what I needed from the practical pieces in my kids' rooms. It opened my mind to another design category that was so fun to explore.

THE BALANCING ACT

My husband and I were very lucky we waited to start a family. We had been married for 11 years and had already laid the foundation, and the groundwork for our company was already made, so creating that balance was easier. I felt strongly about not changing our lives entirely for children but inviting them into the world we had created. I'm so proud to be able to show my children that it is possible to have a rewarding career and a rich family life – it is something we work very hard at every day.

My downtime is about being with my family. I like to travel with my family and expose my children to different places and cultures. It's a joy to see new experiences through their eyes. Family is my greatest achievement. Being a good wife and mother and a good friend is important to me. In my career, being able to empower women to feel confident and beautiful in my clothes has been a huge accomplishment. My advice is to focus on what you're passionate about and to be determined and consistent. Be authentic to who you are, because if you aren't, people can see right through that.

MONIQUE'S TIPS

- *Stay focused on your product and protective of its integrity.*

- *Determination is key.*

- *Value relationships – you can't build a successful business without wonderful partnerships along the way.*

- *Be committed and consistent.*

- *Go with your gut.*

> FIND OUT WHO YOU ARE AND BE THAT PERSON. THAT'S WHAT YOUR SOUL WAS PUT ON THIS EARTH TO BE. FIND THAT TRUTH, LIVE THAT TRUTH AND EVERYTHING ELSE WILL COME.
>
> — ELLEN DEGENERES

JENNIFER FISHER

JEWELLERY ENTREPRENEUR

From Hollywood stylist to mother of two, to jewellery entrepreneur, Jennifer Fisher has proved anything is possible. Starting out in her bedroom, she has grown Jennifer Fisher Jewelry into a multi-million dollar business.

My styling career was a lucky break. I studied Business Marketing at USC with a Fine Arts minor. I was convinced I wanted to work on the advertising side at a fashion magazine. During a brief internship of watching the other interns in the fashion department roll racks of designer clothing by as I was crunching ad numbers, I knew I was on the wrong side of the magazine. I began assisting a few celebrity stylists who, unfortunately, were not the easiest to work for.

As luck would have it, my best friend was working at the time at Propaganda Films under a commercial director who needed a new wardrobe stylist. Timing is truly everything. I took a chance and accepted the job without any commercial styling experience; after my first commercial with him, I became his regular stylist, and we spent the next 10 years working together, taking on major national ad campaigns from American Express to Budweiser. For me, it was more about the larger branded commercials than celebrities. I could book multiple ad campaigns with multiple sets of assistants, and it was an amazing ride. The biggest challenge at this time was managing all the different jobs and travel.

I was diagnosed with my tumour while I was living and styling in NYC for an LA-based director. I had to receive 12 rounds of chemotherapy in Los Angeles at Cedars Sinai and in New York at Saint Vincent's. I worked throughout the entire process. Being diagnosed with anything is always scary, but finding out I had a very rare tumour with no guaranteed form of treatment was the scariest time of my life. It changes everything. From that moment on, your outlook on every day of your life is different.

My husband Kevin proposed to me in the middle of my chemotherapy treatment one night before a big Halloween party at our West Village apartment. We were married a year later – six months after I finished my treatment. When we wanted to have children, my oncologist didn't think it was a good idea for me to carry the baby because my tumour grows from oestrogen – so we went through the process of hiring a surrogate to carry for us in California, where Kevin and I both grew up and our families still live. After multiple rounds of IVF, where the surrogate was pregnant twice and miscarried twice, I came back to New York and decided to try IVF on my own, against my doctor's orders. Unsuccessful yet again, they recommended that we adopt or get an egg donor. We needed a break from it all and took the summer off. That's when I became pregnant with my son Shane, naturally. Against the wishes of my oncologist, I carried the baby. A perfectly healthy pregnancy and baby boy later, we learned that my tumour had actually shrunk from the pregnancy.

CREATING THE BRAND

After Shane was born, I began receiving jewellery gifts to represent him in the form of single letters that were very dainty and, frankly, not my style. His birth was a major deal for Kevin and me, and I wanted something to wear that represented him in a way that felt like me. Being a stylist makes you pretty resourceful, so I went up to 47th Street in the jewellery district in NYC and began knocking on doors, working out how I could create something myself.

My first piece of jewellery was a dog tag to represent my son Shane. After unsuccessfully searching for that ideal piece of jewellery, I had taken it upon myself to make my own. I was wearing the dog tag every day while on set styling and started to get multiple requests for the same necklace. I then happened to make a necklace for Uma Thurman that she ended up wearing on the cover of *Glamour Magazine*. Thus, Jennifer Fisher Jewelry was born.

I started a website selling fine jewellery direct to consumers very early on. This gave the line global reach. I truly believe that the early timing of this coincided with the beginning of the online shopping boom, resulting in a happy accident.

After six years of only selling fine jewellery, I was lucky to have garnered a pretty significant following. In order to offer jewellery to a growing customer base, I decided to expand the line with the launch of the brass collection, focusing on large statement pieces at a more accessible price point. We mainly focus on 14K yellow gold and use a process of lost wax casting for our charms and brass statement pieces. The brass is then plated in 14K yellow gold or silver. We also offer all of our fine pieces in 14K and 18K white, rose and yellow gold. My design process is a bit different than other jewellers as I am inspired by architecture, furniture and lighting design as well as photography.

EXPANDING THE BRAND
Barneys was a combination of the CMO and CEO hearing my name and seeing pictures of my design, and within two days they ended up in my office and picked up the brass line immediately. Net-a-Porter followed soon after. We have been approached by other retailers, but we like to keep our retail distribution tight.

Our celebrity customer base has been amazingly supportive. We have a lot of loyal women who have grown with us and have charm necklaces they have been building with more charms for the past 10 years. However, every day, new customers are discovering us through social media, online and print platforms and now even radio. In terms of utilising social media, I think it is more about being yourself than trying to be an influencer. I have watched my brand increase exponentially when I stopped being someone that I was not supposed to be and was just myself. My biggest challenge has been managing growth. It has been incredibly hard but rewarding to take something that I started in my bedroom and grow it into a multi-million dollar business. Having a second child has also been a challenge, but it is more about scheduling than anything. Obviously, it changes things because your workload doubles, especially when you have children of two different sexes. But it's really no big deal – I have learned it's all about time management!

JENNIFER'S TIPS

- *Don't take no for an answer.*

- *Be nice to everybody.*

- *Focus on what you should be doing and not what other people are doing.*

- *Re-invest your sales back into your business.*

- *Listen to your gut.*

LEESA EVANS

HOLLYWOOD COSTUME DESIGNER AND STYLIST

A sought-after Hollywood stylist and costume designer, Leesa Evans has dressed some of the world's biggest names. She is responsible for helping to create some of the film's most iconic costumes of all time, including the wardrobe of Alicia Silverstone in the film Clueless *and the characters in the films* American Pie *and* Zoolander. *On the red carpet, she's dressed the likes of Rose Byrne and Amy Schumer and is passionate about empowering female characters through costume.*

I have always loved fashion and my mother was a fashion designer when I was young, so there was endless inspiration. My imagination could just run wild. I hadn't originally planned on getting into costume design, but it's been such an incredible career not only for the creative aspects, but I've so enjoyed all the travelling and amazing people I've met along the way.

The film *Clueless* was definitely a turning point for me. It was such a fun project, and it's rare to have an opportunity to mix fashion and film, so I was asked to be the assistant designer because of my background and love of all things fashion. I think the yellow plaid look on Alicia Silverstone's character Cher is probably my favourite and most recognised look from the film. The experience on *Clueless* definitely inspired me to go off on my own and further pursue my career as a costume designer.

After *Clueless*, I did a few smaller films as a costume designer before landing the job on *American Pie*. At that time I was also working as a commercial stylist and private stylist, but I had really become enamoured with the process of building characters and the collaboration required in film-making. So it felt right to really push up my sleeves get to work and make it happen.

It's always a challenge to follow your dreams, especially in a freelance career where there isn't a clear way to get where you want to go. But I had this thought: if I worked hard, I could get there.

THE FILMS
I never had a plan to focus so heavily on comedy. I personally love all genres of film, but there's an amazing family feel working with all the filmmakers in the Judd Apatow camp. Judd has such an incredible ability to see talent, and I am continually impressed by the group he surrounds himself with. It's everyone from the cast to the crew and the creative team. It's been one of my greatest pleasures to work with so many profoundly talented women, such as Kristen Wiig, Rose Byrne, Lena Dunham, Melissa McCarthy, Leslie Mann, Amy Schumer and more. I feel a sense of responsibility in helping empower their characters through clothing to fully support all aspects of the strong, intelligent, funny beautiful women they are so they can tell an authentic story and show their dynamic complexity both on and off screen.

With *Zoolander*, it had always been my dream to use fashion as a character in film. The opportunity to collaborate with so many fashion designers I admire, as well as design my own fashion within the Zoolander film, was truly incredible. The original costume concept was to incorporate 50% couture and 50% comedy into the film, and to me, the perfect example is the lavender rose dress worn by Kristen Wiig's character, Alexanya.

Amy (Schumer) and I met through Judd Apatow just before *Trainwreck* and we genuinely liked each other immediately, but I could tell she wasn't a huge fan of fashion and hadn't yet found what really worked for her. So there was this exciting period of time when I got to introduce her to how good clothing can make you feel and how much fun you can have with it.

I admire Amy and her incredible talent and very generous nature – she is truly a beautiful person inside and out, so often, in dressing her, I want everyone to know what I know and love about her. Amy and I are both attracted to a certain simplicity in her style choices and to me, it feels authentic. I know when there's an effortless tone to her look – it gives her the strength to be all that she is and all that she wants to be without having to feel self-conscious that she's trying to be someone she's not.

MY PHILOSOPHY

My philosophy is to focus on what shapes and silhouettes make someone feel good, strong and confident. I think we all know that feeling when we feel confident in what we're wearing and the result is you have a really great day. What if we could all have that really great day every day? I believe that confidence is more attractive than any one outfit or article of clothing, and the effect of feeling so good daily is an effortlessness in getting dressed. That effortlessness makes you feel happier and then, as a result, kinder, and that level of kindness can change the world.

My absolute favourite part of being a costume designer is coming up with the initial concept for the film. I love the fashion research, to the character development, to visualising the colour palate, to sketching and gathering fabric swatches, to making the character boards. It's the most creative moment of the film for me.

I would say my biggest success is balance, and my biggest challenge has been balance. The film industry can be all-encompassing and leave little time for anything else, so it's been such a huge learning experience to be able to pull back time wise to be able to do everything I want to do in life.

I am inspired by so many people for different reasons: Yves Saint Laurent for his fashion, Malala Yousafzai for her intelligence and bravery, Steve Jobs for his ingenuity, the Dali Lama for spreading love, and the countless women inventors and activists who have paved the way for me to have so many opportunities in life.

I believe a game changer is someone who is committed to forging a new path and creating opportunities for new perspectives. A game changer believes that everything is possible and embraces all challenges in achieving the dream.

GETTING INTO THE INDUSTRY

- There are some amazing film and fashion schools that have costume design programmes.
- Reach out to a costume designer or stylist for an internship.
- Become a production assistant on a commercial or film shoot.
- Contact an extras casting company to work as an extra, and once you are on set before or after work go and speak to the production coordinator and convince them you are smart, resourceful and willing to work hard as a production assistant.
- Contact someone you know who works in film or fashion and ask for an introduction to anyone hiring interns, then work hard and show them you are indispensable.

LEESA'S TIPS

- *All experience is good experience.*

- *Work for people you admire to learn how to do things right as well as wrong.*

- *Fill a void in your field.*

- *Never give up, and always be willing to look at things differently.*

ELEONORA LASTRUCCI

FASHION DESIGNER

Famed Italian fashion designer Eleonora Lastrucci got her start in Italy, working with her father and seeing Roberto Cavalli come in to print his jeans. Since then, she has dressed many actors and celebrities around the world for red-carpet events.

I was a very curious little girl. I loved colours, sequins, I was always drawing. I was attracted by fabrics and started travelling around Europe looking for ideas to make my clothes, and with the help of my father I immediately started working in his company, a fabric printing factory, with a chemical laboratory full of colours that I used in my drawings. They were beautiful years; the passion became a 360-degree job.

CAREER BEGINNINGS

My passion was born at the age of seven. My father had a textile company in Prato where he printed fabrics, and I was born into this large family where you could breathe the smell of fabric, of elegance. I attended the art school in Florence, and while I was studying, I was already working because in the afternoon, at the end of school hours, I went to the company and immediately my drawings were printed on cloth for customers all over Italy.

DESIGNING DRESSES

With a dress, I want to convey to the woman the sense of representation of herself. She must feel beautiful and desired. Fashion is a suggestive idea; every woman has her own natural beauty. The purpose I set for myself, which was also my teenage dream, is to highlight this without however leaving the margins of grace. Elegance, in some cases, is even discretion. It dares to the extent that the shape remains adherent to the sinuosity of a moving body. In Cannes, elegance becomes whimsical, surreal.

CAREER TURNING POINT

I had a special collaboration with a French brand, which opened doors.

CHALLENGES

I was lucky, I had a creative and famous mentor who taught me not to believe in failure. Positivity has helped me to never be depressed or unhappy in my work.

QUALITIES FOR SUCCESS

Success is an abstract thing. To have it you must be prepared to sacrifice your days by dedicating many hours to your work. You have to surround yourself with people who believe in you and make them participate in your work. You have to know how to create quality things.

INSPIRATION

I got to know particular people in the field of fashion, such as Roberto Cavalli, who used to come to our company to print jeans. His knowledge helped me in my work. When I finished my studies, I started working in the same family company, then with Enrico Coveri, a family friend; from him I learned to dare in colours and shapes.

FUTURE ASPIRATIONS

I hope to continue giving beauty to women.

LEGACY

I would like to be remembered for being helpful in doing my job well.

ELEONORA'S ADVICE

- *Ambition.*

- *Determination.*

- *Humility.*

- *Willpower.*

*EVERY PHASE
OF YOUR LIFE
AND CAREER
WILL REQUIRE
A DIFFERENT
YOU.*

MEL ROBBINS

CANDICE LAKE

STYLE EDITOR, MODEL, PHOTOGRAPHER, BLOGGER

Candice Lake is an Australian-born photographer, blogger and model. Her fashion label 'Candidate by Candice Lake' was named on US Vogue's best-dressed list. She is TRESemmé's Global Brand Ambassador and is the Contributing Style Editor at Vogue Australia.

I had always wanted to go to art school when I was younger, although somehow, I ended up at law school. A couple of years into it, I luckily fell into modelling, and everything else went out the window. I met the most extraordinary people and experienced things I would never have had access to without modelling. It was an accelerated life lesson, and it was a few years into it, whilst in between shots on a shoot for *Harper's Bazaar*, that I asked the photographer if I could possibly come with him on his next shoot to assist. That was how I began assisting fashion photographers and transitioned to the other side of the camera whilst gaining a Fine Arts Bachelor's degree. Without modelling, I would never have had these amazing opportunities in photography.

I think that it is an exciting time to be a creative person and to have your own brand. Now more than ever, with the movement of young entrepreneurs and the democratisation of the industry with social media and online accessibility, you can be a photographer, model, blogger, entrepreneur, designer and creative director, all under the umbrella of one brand, which is most exciting.

My biggest challenge has been having a child and wanting to really stop and enjoy the precious and limited time with him in the middle of building a brand. I found this very conflicting personally and professionally, trying to balance the two. I travelled with my son everywhere, so we were never separated in the first year, and I only took on jobs that were really important to me. It ended up being a really positive experience and made me really assess my direction, although, at the time, it was quite difficult. Now, my main aim is that whatever I am putting my energy into, I am giving it 100%. Once I accepted it was about quality and not the quantity of time, our life was a lot richer, and my business flourished.

I learnt pretty early on that nothing just falls in your lap. You have to make it happen and take

advantage of any opportunities you've been given. I work extremely hard to make sure I am pushing myself to produce the best quality of work on every single job I do. I didn't just wake up one day and suddenly shoot for big brands. I hustled, I worked for free for a LONG time, I carried sandbags up and down and then back up sand dunes for photographers, and I learnt not to take no for an answer. I learnt to listen to my gut instinct despite everyone's doubts. When people told me modelling was a waste of time, I knew it would allow me to see the world. And then later when everyone told me I was insane to quit modelling to go back to art school, I knew it was right.

I don't really have any major regrets. I really believe that if even if you fail once, twice or 100 times, you are still moving forward. I believe in learning from all mistakes you make along the way to create more opportunities. If you always act with integrity, you should have no regrets.

Angela Ahrendts has definitely been a big inspiration. I love that she was a pioneer of embracing the digital world and, against all odds, she turned Burberry around from an ageing British icon into one of the fastest-growing global luxury brands in the world. Also my husband – he has such a beautiful mind and is an incredibly talented architect and visionary. He is constantly inspiring and pushing me creatively. It is a real joy to share your life with someone whom you admire greatly.

CANDICE'S TIPS

- *Always do what you're afraid to do. If something seems easy, you're not pushing yourself hard enough.*

- *Listen to your gut instinct, take risks, don't take no for an answer and work your butt off doing something you love.*

ANGELA VENTSEL

FOUNDER AND CEO OF ESTX

High-powered lawyer Angela Ventsel has brought global entrepreneurs success and growth by establishing a digital company in Estonia through estx.

As a young person, my desire to try different options and be courageous and law-abiding by nature led me to study law. It has been an essential part of shaping my values and aspirations in life. My attitude towards the world, people and entrepreneurship continues to guide me today. Early on, I realised that true success is not based only on skills, knowledge and position but also on humanity, gratitude, honesty and the ability to see beyond.

BECOMING A LAWYER

The best thing we can always do for ourselves is to consciously and intentionally plan our lives and grow. My journey in entrepreneurship began with a very conscious decision to quit paid work and be the designer of my own life. As a lawyer, I have learned to handle complex situations and understand legal nuances, so my educational background gave me the impetus to make a decision and a platform to navigate different conditions in the business world.

PATH TO SUCCESS

Personal development and success never happen by themselves. We must always know where we want to go and where we are now to reach our potential. We never become ready by waiting, and to discover our personality and the journey of success, we must discipline ourselves to develop it. Change is the key to success and growth, and our success always depends on our personal growth. At the same time, a significant breakthrough comes with first achieving many small breakthroughs. So do It!.

CHALLENGES

We always have the choice to give up or stand up. I never give up by nature. I always believe in myself. I am my own biggest cheerleader, regardless of the situation and challenges! Setbacks are just stepping stones on our journey from which we can always jump higher and further. Sometimes, it is difficult to see opportunities amid pain, but they are still there. We have to want to see them and look for them because every new challenge is an opportunity to grow as a person. Internal ones always precede external victories, and pain never goes away by waiting or rushing but by working and being disciplined and patient because everything is hard before it becomes easy.

CAREER HIGHLIGHT

As the founder and CEO of the company, I have been committed to the success of estx from its first steps. I have worked on all processes to ensure estx runs smoothly. I like to think of each achievement as part of a larger journey. When starting the more inspiring moments, it was clear how happy entrepreneurs are who can create an EU digital company through the Estonian e-Residency programme, and all this paper-free and remotely, without ever having to visit Estonia. Feedback from e-residents proved to us the viability of our vision and fuelled us to continue.

PASSIONS

We all know that real entrepreneurship is like a sport that requires perseverance, determination and overcoming obstacles. However, every entrepreneur's journey is unique, like every athlete's

track. At the same time, entrepreneurship is also a competition with yourself – constant self-surpassing, development, and balance are critical factors in achieving success without losing yourself. Therefore, to avoid losing myself, I have a natural attitude – a healthy business. For me, it's a balanced lifestyle where business passionately meets sports and self-improvement daily.

DEFINING MOMENT

The defining moment in my career was when I decided to step out of my comfort zone and start my own international company. This decision required courage, perseverance, and continuous self-development, and to date, it has opened the doors to several new opportunities and challenges that have guided and shaped my career. Today was the best decision of my life and the beginning of a journey of possibilities.

FUTURE ASPIRATIONS

The future is full of excitement and ambition – continued growth and development of the company, personal self-development, and opportunities to further expand my skills and knowledge and contribute to the success of the company and the team. And always number one to enjoy quality time with your besties and exercise!

CAREER ADVICE

It is important to constantly learn and develop yourself and create a strong contacts network. Courage and curiosity about life help to discover new possibilities and solutions, while striving for excellence, persistence, and patience lead to success.

ANGELA'S TIPS

- *Enjoy life's journey. Without enjoyment, one cannot get far in life.*

- *Be brave. Brave individuals always have more opportunities in life.*

- *Don't fear failure. Challenges open new doors in life.*

- *Invest in yourself. Opportunities always grow with self-improvement.*

- *Take risks. No risk, no win in business and life.*

- *Never give up. You're stronger than you think. Just stand up!*

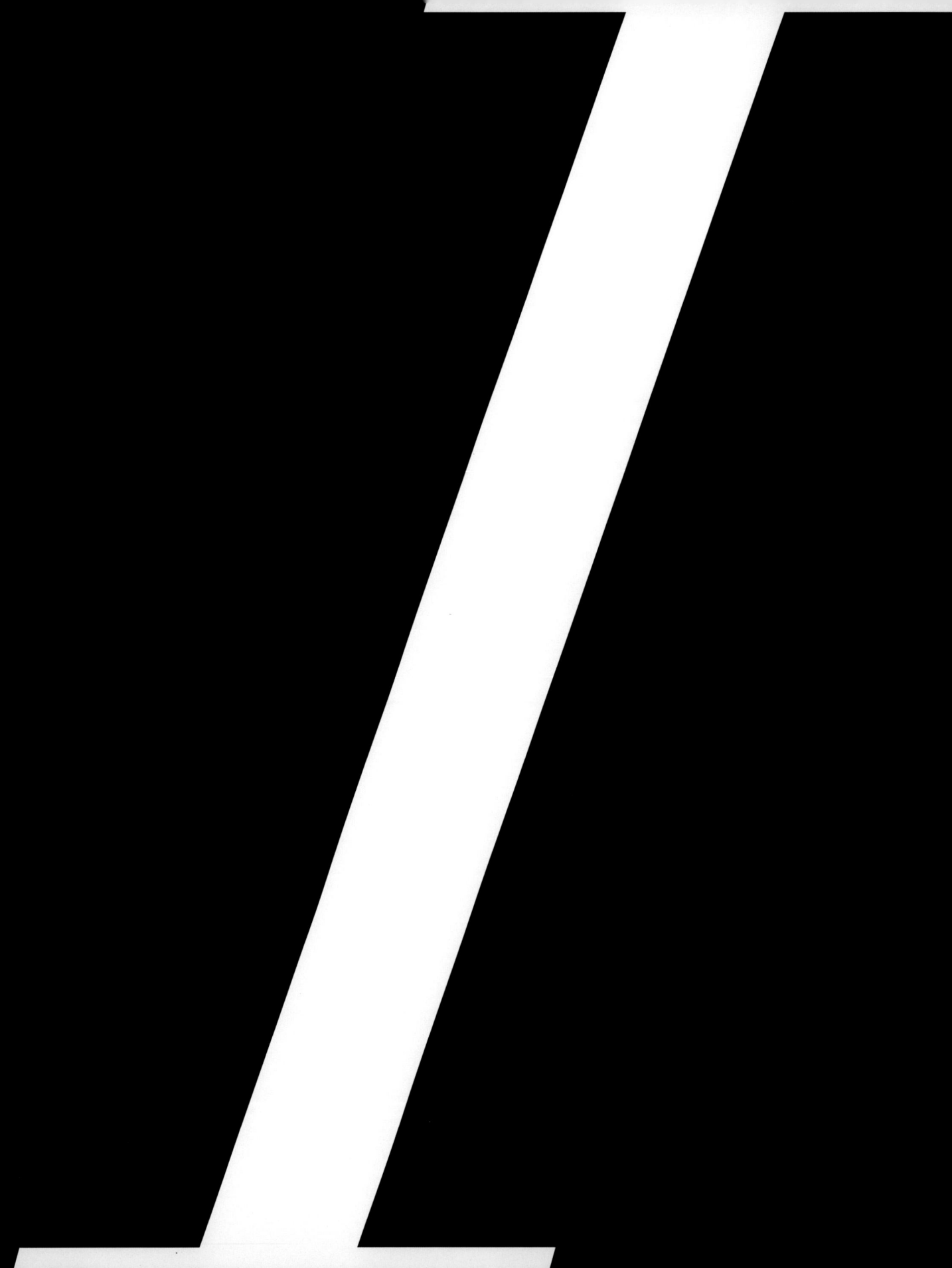

IF YOU ARE SUCCESSFUL, IT IS BECAUSE SOMEWHERE, SOMETIME, SOMEONE GAVE YOU A LIFE OR AN IDEA THAT STARTED YOU IN THE RIGHT DIRECTION.

HELENE BENHAMOU

SINGER

Helene is a famed singer based in Paris who has sung across many TV stations and to live audiences.

STARTING IN YOUR INDUSTRY
In all my careers in the fashion industry, I have believed in myself, I had a vision that I follow religiously. I never pay attention to what people say or think. I follow my gut feeling and believe that everything is possible.

I started this new singing career during the first confinement of the pandemic. I started to sing on Instagram to amuse my friends; that's how it all started. I took singing classes during confinement because I always like to improve myself and become excellent in what I do. Someone suggested to me to have my own song. I thought it was a good idea, but I never thought it would lead me this far.

FASHION EVOLVING IN YOUR CAREER
My style remained the same but became a bit more extravagant because of my TV appearances. It is my signature.

I felt my career really started when I put up my first YouTube video clip for my new song 'Just be you'. From that came many TV producers who contacted me for live TV segments.

You should always feel happy with what you wear. I need to be comfortable and wear something that matches my personality.

CAREER CHALLENGES
I thought that because of my age it was going to be more difficult to succeed. I then realised it was a real advantage. I have no competition!

HOW DO YOU FEEL PEOPLE ARE INFLUENCED BY STYLE?
People are mainly influenced by fashion. I don't follow fashion. I follow my style. Of course, I get influenced by what's new in fashion and then I decide what goes with my style.

WHEN DO YOU FEEL YOUR HAPPIEST?
When I have major TV producers contact me to be on their shows. It is really incredible; it took two years to succeed and to be able to arrive where I am today.

WHO HAS INSPIRED YOU IN THE FASHION INDUSTRY?
I love to look, but nobody influences me. I have my style and I don't like to be influenced.

FASHION ADVICE
Wear something that makes you happy. Wear something that pleases you and not others. Be sure of yourself, love what you wear, choose your outfit depending on your mood.

Be yourself. Follow your dreams. Working hard is not enough; you have to work very, very hard. Good is not an option, only excellence. Be more adventurous by choosing new looks. Choose great accessories.

The way you look is your signature and shows your personality.

KOUKLA LAPIDUS

FRENCH ACTOR

STARTING IN THE FASHION INDUSTRY
I started when I was 17, when I was doing an internship at *Figaro Magazine.* I was walking through the corridor, and Christophe Brunnquell saw me and made me do a casting for a Japanese magazine. Three months later I got the job, and that's how it began.

CAREER CHALLENGE
I've faced challenges because I don't have the measurements that the modelling industry requests, but this didn't stop me from doing covers and shows in Milan.

WALKING RED CARPET
I have worked with Chopard for the last three years at Cannes Film Festival. I work with my stylist Mickael Carpin, and he does magic with my looks.

MY STYLE
Being me. I like to wear something that I feel most comfortable in. I never go shopping in Paris; I prefer to find the vintage, 'Année 2000' kind of clothes. Sometimes they come from Australia, so I need to be patient before I can wear them. The product and feel of the clothes are more important for me than the brand. I am always inspired by old movies to dress up.

FASHION INFLUENCE
I think we are all influenced by someone and that's beautiful, the mix of an inspiration and touch of you.

STYLE AND CAREER
I think the style can be a power to show who you are. It doesn't make everything but it's a big part of you. That little '*je ne sais quoi, ce presque rien*'.

CAREER HIGHLIGHT
I'm proud of the Sunglasshut Campaign in Times Square that I did with my sister Milla. Sharing this with my sister makes it even more special for me.

ADVICE FOR SUCCESS IN FASHION
No one is allowed to tell you that you shouldn't do it. If you believe in it, you should go for it. Don't be afraid. The only thing that matters is that you are feeling good about yourself and not to let anyone change that about you. It's easier to say than to do, but once I understood this, I really started to live.

POWER OF SOCIAL MEDIA
I think social media helps new brands to be more famous; also, we are able to discover new designers.

DEFINE SUCCESS ON YOUR OWN TERMS, ACHIEVE IT BY YOUR OWN RULES, AND BUILD A LIFE YOU ARE PROUD TO LIVE.

ANNE SWEENEY

NATALIE DE'BANCO

CREATIVE DIRECTOR OF BRONX AND BANCO

Natalie De'Banco is a fashion designer based in New York who has dressed celebrities such as Beyoncé, J-Lo, Miley Cyrus and Alicia Keys.

STARTING IN THE FASHION INDUSTRY

It all started when I was three years old, playing with my grandmother's button collection. Then, during my college years I started my own re-sale business on eBay where I would buy, alter and re-sell clothing. It got so successful that it grew into a pop-up store in the neighbourhood where I lived in Sydney, Australia. From there, I went on to study fashion at a business level, at which time Channel 9 (the local news station in Bondi Beach) reached out to me to custom pieces for their team. This ultimately inspired me to build a brand of my own.

BUILDING A GLOBAL BRAND

Slowly and painfully! First, I moved to Turkey and spent a year doing production. This had its challenges; there was an obvious language barrier and since it is an all-male dominated country, it felt a little intimidating and uncomfortable to accomplish what I wanted to. I decided to redirect and take my production to Asia. I learned the language, interned at a factory for a little bit and then opened my own factory. Next step was to partner with international agents while I looked after the design and production. Along with this, one factor that really helped with brand exposure was showing during fashion weeks – this generated buzz around the brand, and we got picked up by publications, celebrities and department stores.

Bronx and Banco is now stocked in Bergdorf Goodman, Saks Fifth Avenue, Neiman Marcus, Bloomingdales, Revolve and more. The greatest challenge was building the right relationships to get into these stores in the first place. Then, once you're in, you must keep your finger on the pulse, making sure you have the right merchandise for your customer who changes her mind from season to season. The rest is history in the making!

CHALLENGES

People say fashion is one of the most challenging industries, and there is a reason for that. We've seen a lot of copies of our designs since our brand has become popular, and finding a way to copyright and keep our designs safe is something we have struggled with. Another big challenge the brand

faced was moving the business to America from Australia. Being from a different country and having to integrate into a new world felt like starting from scratch all over again. You sort of always feel like the new kid on the block. Across the board, the fashion industry holds its challenges, but this is what makes you resilient.

WORKING WITH CELEBRITIES
The brand has always done a lot of custom work for celebrities such as Beyoncé, J-Lo, Miley Cyrus, Mary J. Blige, Alicia Keys and Kelly Rowland. We have strong relationships with our stylists, some of which have lasted since the brand's beginnings. Being asked to be part of 'Queen B's' *Renaissance* album art and visuals back in 2021 was beyond exciting. Once we built those relationships and saw how well the brand aligned with the vision the team had for *Renaissance*, they asked us to create custom pieces for her tour. Working together with the team and creating something so special was a dream come true.

SOCIAL MEDIA
Social media is an amazing way to organically grow your network and keep the world connected to your brand. We also use it as a direct sense of communication, making sure we are keeping our customers updated and communicating directly with our influencers or stylists. It's also an amazing way to track trends and see where fashion is heading overall.

NATALIE'S ADVICE

- *It's important to decide where you want to place yourself in the fashion industry – the business side or creative side (or both) that will help you decide what steps to take.*

- *Whether you are at the beginning of your career or pivoting in your career, it is important to stay relevant by taking courses. Even after 20 years in the industry, I am constantly using resources to educate myself.*

KRISTINA BAZAN

SOCIAL INFLUENCER, CREATOR OF KAYTURE.COM

Kristina Bazan is wise beyond her years. She launched her fashion and beauty blog, Kayture.com, five years ago and has already amassed more than two million followers, is a L'Oréal Paris Brand Ambassador, has been featured in Forbes 30 Under 30 and has appeared on the cover of Vogue Portugal. *She has forayed into music and even written a book,* On the Go, *all while in her early twenties.*

I was 17 years old and still in high school when I realised that creativity was in my bones and that I had always wanted to do so many different things with my life, and what better a time to start! I had a boyfriend who was in photography and he started taking editorial photos of me. We sent out some of the pictures to an agent, who convinced us that we should keep going.

LOOKBOOK.nu was a popular social media platform at the time. I began using it, posting my 'photos of the day', and I started getting a lot of traction. At the time I was living in a tiny village in Switzerland where the average age is 60 years old. I had cows and goats in the front of my house. There was one bus every hour. It was kind of miserable and boring. So all of a sudden, being able to have a hobby was really fun for me. Six months after posting photos, somehow *Vogue* heard about me, my photos and what James and I were doing. I got invited to an event in Tokyo, where I realised that there was a lot of potential in what we were doing. So James put together a business plan with the aim of creating a company. Honestly, my first goal was to be able to sustain myself – and also convince my parents not to make me go to college! It is a scary thing to dive into the blue, and we definitely needed something consistent.

BUILDING THE BRAND
Our business plan was pretty simple: to create editorials that you would see in the likes of *Vogue* magazine. After all, *French Vogue* was my bible. But it always seemed extremely unrelatable – no girl can technically afford the outfits featured in the pages, and so I always managed to find stuff at Zara or vintage items, and make it look like it was in a magazine through styling. Our plan was to basically make editorials – just James and I. We focused on creating iconic, beautiful images with the aim

of inspiring a large community of people. We had no makeup artist, no lighting, no fancy sets – just images that we hoped would be more relatable to the women who started to follow us. It seemed to work, because big brands got interested in us super-quickly, while so many women started wanting to shop for the stuff I was wearing. The brand grew organically – we kept producing images, and the followers kept on coming. The interest just grew and grew.

The social media landscape is changing so quickly, and it's kind of scary! I focused on being innovative – not so much on growing my followers, but rather on creating quality content because that is what is going to last. Of course, it is good to have a lot of followers, but it is better to inspire a conversation and engage with the readers. The motto that I stick by is that every post needs to be top-notch in quality.

There is a lot of speculation about how we make money and whether we just post anything for the sake of it. But that is not true. For me, the most important thing I have learnt is to be very picky in regards to my projects. My main income comes from choosing the right partners and creating long-term projects. L'Oréal is one of the main ones right now, and we now have about 10-15 partners that we do regular projects with, rather than saying 'yes' to everything. It gives us a certain power – to be able to choose what we want to accept. This also allows me to say no to a lot of things. Of course, when you have salaries to pay and a team to look after, you have to make sure you have enough cash flow!

One of my favourite projects to work on has been with Mugler – as they allowed me to art direct the whole thing. I created the whole video concept with my best friend for three different fragrances. I even got to write a song for it and did a huge promotion on my end. They trusted me so much on everything, and that is what I love – working with incredible brands on big projects becomes bigger than social media and blog posts. At the moment it's important for me to evolve and establish myself more and more, not just throughout my blog, but outside social media. I'm extremely passionate about art directing outside the blog, working for brands and magazines, and creating editorials. Music is also a big part of my time. I am putting together new music for my album, which I am super passionate about and want to let that grow organically.

Several years ago, when I was still living in Switzerland, I had a French editor reach out to me asking me to share my stuff with an international audience, which is how my first book came about, *On The Go*. It was a lot of fun putting together and something I am very proud of.

HOW TO BE A SOCIAL INFLUENCER
Try to emulate your own success and figure out what you're good at. I think we all have something very special to share, and it's important to figure out what it is and try to make a good impact. I'm still figuring out what I want my impact to be, but I definitely don't want to confine myself to only blogging. I think it's almost too shallow at times. I want to use my influence and voice to spread a message on work ethics and to encourage young women to create their own system: to inspire women (and men as well) to pursue their passions even if they have social pressures from family and friends to do something else. I am grateful to do something of my own, and it's good to be reminded that no matter what you do – "True passion is what matters."

KRISTINA'S TIPS

- *Always create top-notch quality posts.*

- *Have an art concept.*

- *Try to target the right people.*

- *Be aware of who you're talking to.*

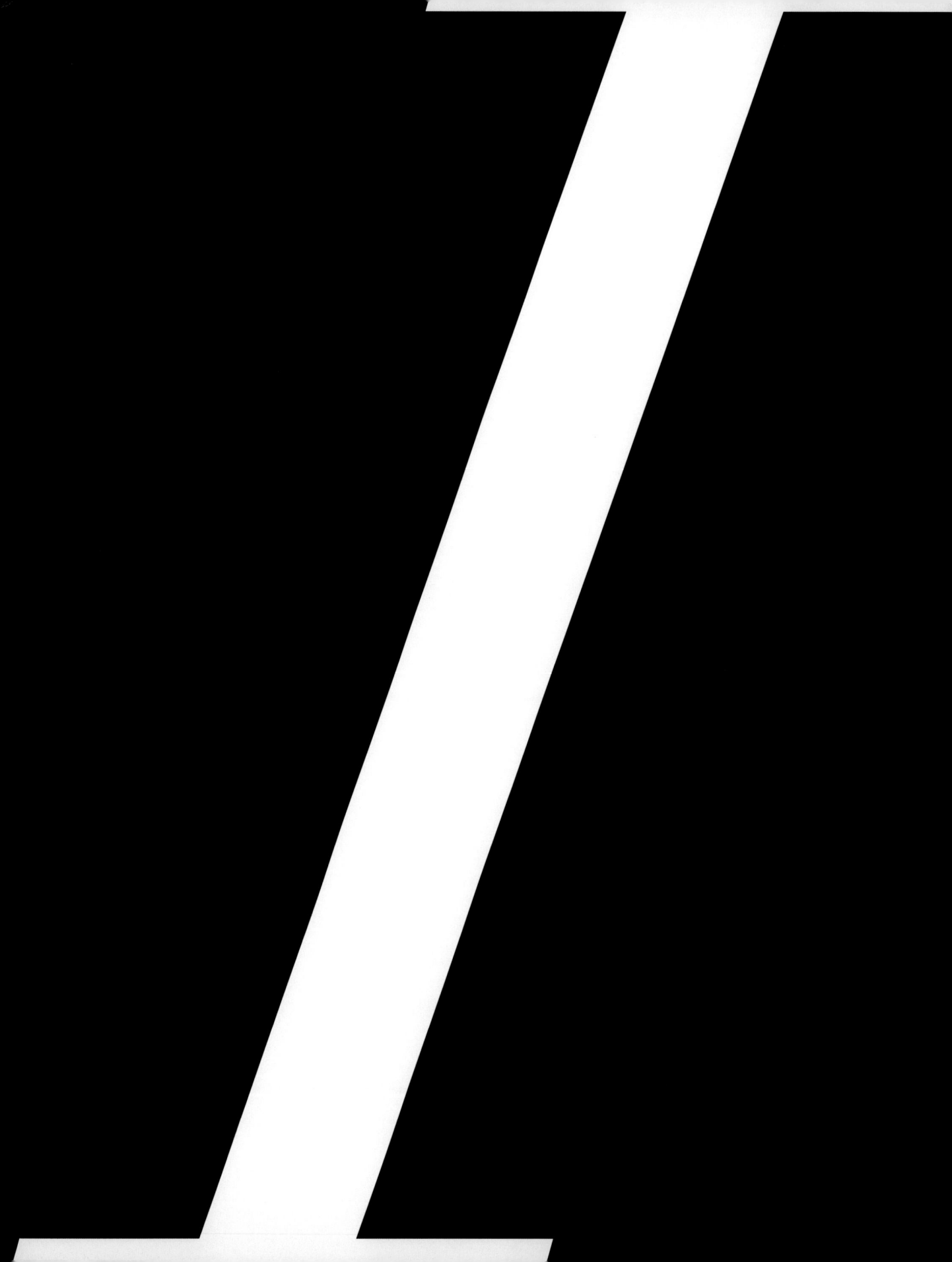

DONE BEFORE. GROWTH AND COMFORT DO NOT CO-EXIST.

VIRGINIA ROMETTY (CEO OF IBM)

MEGAN HESS

INTERNATIONAL FASHION ILLUSTRATOR

Megan Hess is an international fashion illustrator and has been called upon by some of the most prestigious fashion designers and luxury brands around the world, including Chanel, Prada, Dior and Louis Vuitton. In 2008, she illustrated the bestselling book Sex and The City *by Candace Bushnell. Her works can now be seen at leading hotels, in numerous books and on the walls of global fashion houses. She is the creative patron for the Ovarian Cancer Research Foundation.*

I studied Graphic Design because it felt like a 'real' job in the art world, but I really always wanted to be an illustrator – I just never knew back then that it was a possible career choice! After working as an art director in advertising agencies for several years, I packed everything up and moved from Australia to London. It was in London that I worked in a million different creative jobs and in my final job there, I realised that I had a burning desire to be an artist.

At this time, I became the Art Director for Liberty Department Store. Whist I loved art-directing fashion, I loved illustrating it more. I started to do very small illustrations for Liberty, and from this, art directors saw my work and little commissions began to follow.

After about a year I found myself with non-stop work. I wasn't earning a fortune, but I'd never been happier and I knew I was going to do this forever.

As my clients got bigger and better, I was able to be a little more selective and just work on briefs that I knew had a great creative opportunity. Then in 2006, I got a call in the middle of the night from Candace Bushnell's publisher, asking if I would illustrate her next novel *One Fifth Avenue*. This was when things took off at rapid speed for me. Her book became a *New York Times* bestseller. I later met with Candace, and she asked me to illustrate all her previous books, including the cover of *Sex and the City*. Once *Sex and the City* was released, I was contacted by *TIME* magazine in New York to create portraits for them. This was a dream come true, and I still can't believe I work for them. Following this, I began illustrating for Tiffany & Co, Chanel, Dior, Cartier, Vanity Fair, Italian Vogue, Bergdorf Goodman, Prada, Salvatore Ferragamo.... Ironically, at the same time as my work finally took off, I had my first baby! It's funny, I always tell people that I haven't really slept since 2006!

THE CHALLENGES

The biggest challenge has been managing it all! In the very beginning, the struggle was to find great projects to work on. I initially had no clients and I wasn't yet a mother then, so the challenge was to get things moving. Then once my work took on after *Sex and the City* I had the opposite problem – I had lots of great projects and brands coming to me to collaborate and I also had just had a baby, so it was quite overwhelming.

Today, I still find the biggest challenge juggling it all. I can now only take on about 20% of the jobs that come to me each year, so I have to be very careful about what projects are the best – I've learnt that it's better to do a smaller amount of jobs at 100% then lots of jobs at 50%. At the end of the day, I try to base this decision on what projects will have the best creative outcome – some projects have huge budgets and others are tiny, but I always choose to work on projects that will fulfil me creatively.

I've always believed that ability will only get you so far and attitude, however, is everything. I think that in the very beginning (before *Sex and the City*), I gave 100% to every single illustration job that came my way. Most of the projects that came to me in the very begging were NOT inspiring. For example, I was asked to illustrate a 300-page horse manual that on completion was cancelled! After six months of work, I received a tiny 'kill fee' and really felt like giving up on my dream of becoming a fashion illustrator. Another soul-destroying job that almost made me give up was a pizza toppings illustration for a pizza company. I remember very clearly the day I finished drawing that – I turned off the light in my studio at the end of the day and thought to myself. "I think it's time to give up." That very night, at 3am, was when I received the call from Candace Bushnell's publisher and my life changed forever. In short, I think never giving up is the biggest lesson I've learnt.

I feel my biggest achievement is getting paid to do what I love for a living, and being a mother. I see it as a huge luxury to be able to do both, and it's something that I'm very grateful for every day. I've also been able to donate many pieces of my work to charities and causes all over the world and in some small way, I feel proud that one of my drawings may have helped someone somewhere. As Creative Patron of Ovarian Cancer, I've also had the privilege of working with the most inspiring team of people trying to raise awareness and funds for the development of an early-detection test for Ovarian Cancer.

INSPIRATIONS

My parents were always very supportive of my dreams and always made me feel like anything was possible. In high school, I had an amazing art teacher who helped build a sense of confidence in me to pursue drawing. Later in life, I have really been inspired by so many other creative people all over the world who I have worked with. I learnt to take advice, to really listen and see what makes other people interesting or creative. Even people who are difficult or demanding to work with; there is still always knowledge to be gained by the experience of working together. Above all, I have learnt that no matter what anyone else feels, you have to go with your gut.

One of my favourite collaborations has been with Tiffany & Co in New York. I was asked to illustrate their iconic 5th Avenue building filled with chic Tiffany & Co people in the foreground! It was dream project. Another collaboration that was wonderful to work on was with Cartier in Paris. It all centred around Paris Fashion Week, and I created 10 bespoke illustrations for their Paris Nouvelle Vague Collection.

Most recently, I collaborated with Prada in Milan on an animation for their Autumn Winter Collection – the creative process of that job was probably one of the most exciting. In terms of individuals, I have worked on some very exciting (and nerve-wracking) portraits – everyone from Gwyneth Paltrow and Jennifer Lopez to Michelle Obama.

GLOBAL REACH

Working globally continues to be a challenge. Today, it's probably one of the things that I love most about what I do because it's incredibly exciting to work with different brands and projects all over the world. The problem initially was that all my work was coming from New York and Europe, and communicating and travelling with a newborn baby was very hard! Even if I wasn't travelling, I was always Skyping late at night and early in the morning and then illustrating all day long – it was very hard to have any time to switch off. Now, I have my communicating with overseas down to a fine art. For all my US clients, I wake at 6am – I do my makeup and hair in six minutes – I keep my PJs on the bottom half and wear something chic on the top half (because that's all they can see on Skype), then I do the Skype before my kids are even awake. Then I'm off to my day. I'll then do a late-night Skype the next night to Europe – but never the two on the same day. I also condense my travelling to what is really necessary. Everything is planning. If I can really hone the schedule of any work trip, it becomes both productive and enjoyable.

I did find the juggling of all the projects that I work on very overwhelming at times. Even though I was working on many 'dream projects', the stress of getting it all done could outweigh the joy that I should have felt. The greatest thing that I did to combat that stress was learn to meditate. In the beginning, it was so hard to quieten the mind – it felt impossible. But I didn't give up on it, and once it clicked and began working, it changed my life. Initially, I could only do 10 minutes, but now I can easily do 20 minutes of meditation, and it feels like I've completely recharged my battery. It's really made me feel like I can tackle any issue without stress, and to me that's a very powerful thing.

MEGAN'S TIPS

- *Decide what is the one thing that would make you excited to spring out of bed on a Monday morning and do that for a career.*

- *Write down a plan and strategy to make that dream happen and start on it today.*

- *You don't need to suddenly quit your current job or dramatically change your life, but taking the first step is always the hardest.*

- *Never, ever give up on that dream. If it's something that you love, then you will enjoy the process, regardless of the outcome.*

ELLA MILLS

BESTSELLING AUTHOR AND HEALTH ENTREPRENEUR

Ella Mills is an award-winning author. She writes the popular website Deliciously Ella, and is a champion of eating well. Her first book has been the bestselling debut cookbook ever in the UK, an Amazon bestseller, a New York Times *bestseller and has been translated into 15 languages. She's since written three more bestsellers.*

Before I became ill, back in 2011, I was studying History of Art at St Andrews University. I was a normal student and was looking to work within the art world. In June that year, I suddenly got ill, and that changed everything. After months in hospital, having test after test, I was diagnosed with Postural Tachycardia Syndrome, a chronic illness that affects the autonomic nervous system, stopping it from working as it should – so I couldn't regulate my heart rate, circulation, digestion and immune system, amongst other issues. I tried conventional medicine for about six months, but sadly this didn't help as much as I had hope,d and I was still bed-ridden most of the time. That's when I decided to look at diet and lifestyle as tools for managing the symptoms and looked towards a natural, plant-based approach. It took me about 18 months to start getting my symptoms under control and come off my medication and a further year or two on top of that to feel pretty normal.

THE CHALLENGES

Overcoming my illness was so hard for me, both mentally and physically. As well as the everyday physical challenges, I really struggled with depression and isolation. I struggled to keep going and push forward at this time, and although the end results were positive, it absolutely wasn't uphill all the way – I'd have so many bad days when I was fighting so hard for good ones, which was a real challenge. Likewise, I made progress in some areas, but others took a long time to see any change, and I still have to be careful to manage the condition. This can be hard, as it does still mean daily limitations, but I can really live my life now.

CREATING DELICIOUSLY ELLA

I'm so lucky that Deliciously Ella happened very organically. I started the blog as a way of me teaching myself how to cook and to document what I was learning. It's come a long way since then. I've now written four books, launched a best-selling app, opened two delis in London and launched a product line into stores across the UK.

I think when it comes to creating a brand around yourself, being authentic is the most important aspect. You have to embrace who you are and share that. People see straight through fake personalities – especially in the world of social media. I think it is just sheer determination, confidence in what you're doing and a real passion for what you do. It's important to develop a tough skin, too: criticism is really important for growth, so we all need to learn to embrace negative comments and learn from them, and at the same time, learn when to tune it out.

As we've grown into more areas, it's been so important to stay true to the core values of Deliciously Ella. This is something that we work on every day to ensure that they're consistent across all our projects.

I couldn't have built what I have without the people around me, though; finding a strong team is everything. I really believe a business is only as good as the people in it, and I've learnt so much from everyone I'm lucky enough to work with.

ELLA'S TIPS

- *Be genuine, authentic and yourself. Find your voice and be consistent with it, and always engage with your audience.*

- *Drop your ego and surround yourself with fantastic people who can help you drive your vision forward. Learn from them, listen to the criticism and don't be afraid to admit when you're wrong.*

- *Never give up, and always be an optimist. Everyone wants to quit sometimes, but the people who succeed are the ones that keep pushing through. See the daily challenges as learning curves that make you better, so that you keep growing.*

AMANDA HARRIGAN

FOUNDER OF GLOBAL MATCHMAKING SERVICE HYTCH

Amanda Harrigan is the founder of global matchmaking service Hytch, which helps their clients to find meaningful connections.

Growing up, my dad was deeply invested in personal development. I remember him listening to Brian Tracy tapes and reading books about the power of the mind and subconscious in shaping one's dreams. When he passed those books and tapes on to me, I became fascinated with psychology and human behaviour, immersing myself in these subjects throughout my teenage years.

In 2000, I came across an article in the *Sydney Morning Herald* about the emerging field of life coaching and the transformative impact life coaches had on people's lives. Instantly, I knew that this was my calling and that I wanted to help others achieve their goals and transform their lives.

LAUNCHING MY COMPANY

After completing my Life Coaching Certification in 2004, I attended a seminar on relationships that emphasised the connection between our relationship with ourselves and our relationships with others. This resonated deeply with me, leading me to further studies and to specialise in life and relationship coaching.

In 2012, I launched my coaching business, Emotive Health. That same year, a friend who had recently returned from Europe and the U.S. introduced me to the matchmaking industry. I was intrigued by the idea of helping people find meaningful relationships and, after researching the Australian market, I saw a huge opportunity. At the time, many Australians were unfamiliar with professional matchmaking.

This realisation led me to establish my first exclusive matchmaking agency, Platinum Introductions, in 2013. However, I soon discovered that matchmaking required far more than my coaching experience, it was an intricate process with its own complexities and nuances. Despite my enthusiasm, I lacked the specialised knowledge needed to make it a success.

To truly master the art of matchmaking, I spent the next four and a half years working with an established matchmaker. This experience gave me a solid foundation, helping me understand the intricacies of matching people for lasting romantic relationships.

INSPIRATION

After years of working in the industry and researching the Australian market, I identified a major opportunity to create a premium matchmaking service unlike anything available. I studied the most successful agencies in the UK and U.S., refining my approach to bring an elevated, high-calibre experience to Australia.

In 2020, I launched Hytch, a private and exclusive matchmaking service tailored to professionals, executives, and business owners seeking meaningful, long-term relationships. I built Hytch on the foundation of everything I had learned, leveraging my past challenges, insights, and industry experience to create a service designed for discerning clients who value privacy, exclusivity, and quality matches.

CHALLENGES

Unlike Europe and the U.S., where matchmaking is widely recognised as the preferred way for high-achieving individuals to find partners, Australia was still unfamiliar with the industry. Many people didn't realise that a private, exclusive service like Hytch was exactly where high-calibre individuals were turning to find meaningful connections.

The challenges I faced with Platinum Introductions and my experience working with the other matchmaking firm proved invaluable. They taught me the common pitfalls in the industry, allowing me to develop strategies that have made Hytch a success today.

Understanding the nuances of the business such as client expectations, relationship dynamics, and the importance of discretion, has been instrumental in positioning Hytch as a leader in the field.

LAUNCHING HYTCH

When launching Hytch, I combined my extensive matchmaking experience with my expertise in marketing and branding. I knew that branding, privacy, and exclusivity were essential for my clientele, and I built Hytch with those principles at its core. Many of my professional peers expressed that they would use a service like Hytch if it focused on quality over quantity which was something dating apps lacked.

CLIENTS OF HYTCH

Hytch has had many successful matches of clients aged thirty to eighty. This has resulted in marriages, engagements, babies, couples moving overseas together and moving in together.

Seeing my clients build lasting relationships and hearing their stories of finding true love through Hytch brings me immense joy and fulfilment.

I know I am living my purpose, helping people find love in a world where meaningful connections are becoming harder to find and increasingly rare.

COMPANY VALUES

At Hytch, authenticity is key. We carefully select our clients, ensuring they are genuinely seeking a long-term relationship. Our clients lead healthy, fulfilling lives, and we prioritise compatibility by evaluating personality, values, lifestyle, interests, goals, physical appearance, and overall energy.

Every introduction is made with intention, ensuring our clients are matched with partners who Align With Their Relationship Goals.

CAREER TURNING POINT

A pivotal moment in my career was when two internationally renowned matchmaking firms reached out to me. After researching the Australian market, they identified Hytch as the agency most aligned with their brand and values, and invited me to collaborate for their Australian VIP clients. It was an incredible honour, especially since these were the very agencies I had admired when I first started Hytch.

CAREER ADVICE

Becoming a matchmaker is not just about love and happy relationships, it requires a deep understanding of human psychology, emotional intelligence, and relationship dynamics. The ability to guide people on their dating and relationship journey is fundamental to success in this field.

For those aspiring to enter the industry, I highly recommend gaining experience by working with an established matchmaker and obtaining professional certifications. Continuous education and a commitment to personal growth are essential. Above all, passion is the driving force, you must be truly invested in helping people find love to thrive in this career.

REFLECTIONS

Looking back on my journey, I see how every challenge and setback led me to where I am today. Hytch is more than just a matchmaking service, it's a mission to help professionals find deep, lasting connections.

I am grateful to be part of my clients' love stories and to witness the transformative power of meaningful relationships.

AMANDA'S ADVICE

- *Resilience.*

- *Belief in yourself and your abilities.*

- *Embrace your uniqueness - it's your superpower.*

- *Courage to take risks, even after failure.*

PIA COOKE

HEAD OF ADVISORY SOLUTIONS, GLOBAL WEALTH MANAGEMENT

Pia Cooke is a highly experienced financial professional, with a strong track record of achievement across investment banking, private banking and wealth management. She has twenty-two years of experience working internationally across London, Singapore and Australia.

I grew up on a rural property in Australia, where our nearest neighbour was many kilometres away. It was a wonderful childhood filled with simple pleasures, such as horse riding, playing sports and caring for my wide array of pets, from lambs and cows to even a kangaroo.

This has shaped my perspectives on life today. I cherish simplicity and take nothing for granted. I also developed a strong work ethic from my family. Broadacre farming requires hard, physical work. You need to be multi-skilled, adaptable and willing to roll up your sleeves to get things done. It also has tough times, which teaches resilience and the ability to navigate through life's challenges.

I'm a proud mum of three wonderful kids who've taught me meaningful lessons about happiness and the importance of work-life balance. Over the past two decades, I've immersed myself in the dynamic world of banking, having the privilege of working across three continents in different roles and enjoying diverse cultures and perspectives along the way.

BUILDING MY CAREER

It may seem an unusual leap to go from farming into banking. However, I was always interested in maths and investing, so it was a more natural transition than you might think.

After graduating with a Business degree at university and travelling for a while, my first role was in asset management in Sydney. I spent my days reconciling balance sheets. As I'm sure you can imagine, this lacked excitement for a young, ambitious career girl looking for adventure.

After a year, I got a lucky break. I got the chance to interview some exceptional individuals, who recognised my potential and offered me a chance to join their team. This was the turn of the millennium, 2000, and this propelled me into the world of trading floors and investment banking. I couldn't have asked for a better initiation, and am grateful for those first formative years with the team.

In my career, I've always been driven by a deep commitment to my clients, building lasting relationships founded on trust and integrity.

Grounded by my Australian roots, I bring a down-to-earth approach to my work, believing that genuine connections and empathy are keys to success.

DEFINING MOMENT

I began my career on a trading floor in an investment bank filled with loud voices, lots of screens, and a lot of pressure. Equity derivatives were my speciality. You woke up every morning listening to the news – you knew it would be a good day if the Dow Jones was up. A good day meant making money for the bank. A bad day meant losses, and you could cut the air with a knife. I learnt many life lessons working 'in the trading pit' and am grateful for the years I spent learning about the world of derivatives from my more seasoned colleagues.

The turning point of my career was the Global Financial Crisis. The trading division went from having an enormously profitable business to a struggle for survival overnight, as financial markets faced unprecedented turmoil and uncertainty following the Lehman Brothers bankruptcy. This was 2008. I had never experienced anything like this and hope to never again. Stress levels were sky-high, and for everyone, it was extremely difficult.

Six months later, I moved to Asia, moved into private banking, and never set foot on an investment banking trading floor again. This was a pivotal turning point in my career.

CHALLENGES

All jobs will likely pose moments of challenge, whether it be long hours, periods of stress, or being faced with strategic decisions that are difficult. I currently work in Asia and oversee a wide range of markets. I really enjoy the diversity of the people I work with from Asia, Africa, the UK and UAE and embrace the unique nuances that each market possesses.

My greatest challenge is ensuring I allocate enough time to my family. I'm so pleased to see the banking industry evolving and encouraging more people to work from home at least a few days a week. Twenty years ago, this was unheard of. Today, despite working long hours and typically being in the office early, I always find ways to prioritise my family. Even if this means coming home to spend dinner with them and then logging on after they've gone to bed.

When Covid-19 struck in 2020, I lived in Asia. Borders were closed, personal freedoms were taken away, and I felt incredibly isolated from my family in Australia. For three years, we were unable to be together, and during this period, my mother passed away. While countless people endured similar losses during the pandemic, the passing of my mother was deeply personal and profoundly heart-wrenching. This really changed my perspective on life. I take nothing for granted now. Life is precious and short. I try to cherish every moment, pursue what I love, and try to leave a positive impact on those and the world around me.

QUALITIES FOR SUCCESS

- A strong work ethic. Be willing to work hard, especially early on in your career.

- Have the resilience to overcome obstacles and bounce back. Your career will have setbacks from time to time. Learn from failures. You'll be better and stronger for it.

- Embrace change. The world is becoming exponentially more dynamic, and employees and organisations need to adapt. Be willing to embrace change. We all know what happened to Blockbuster and Kodak.

- Be curious. Ask questions. Learn about things that interest you. Curiosity promotes innovation, drives problem-solving and is essential for success. This is the number one trait I look for when hiring people in my team.

- Constantly look for ways to improve yourself – I once worked for Australia's largest investment bank, and I was given some great advice by my friend, the Head of HR. "If you're not moving forward, you're moving backwards." Simply put, this means: always invest in yourself, learn new things and stay relevant in a dynamic, rapidly changing world.

INSPIRATION

We all draw inspiration from different sources. When I first began in banking, it was a male-dominated industry. I drew inspiration from successful investors who led incredible companies, such as Warren Buffet, chairman and CEO of Berkshire Hathaway. I truly admired his investment acumen, but also his humility, integrity and strong ethics.

In later years, I've come to admire many of the women who have forged remarkable careers in my industry, such as Jane Fraser, CEO of Citigroup, the first and only female CEO on Wall Street; Samara Cohen, the Chief Investment Officer of Blackrock's ETF and Index business: and Sallie Krawcheck, former Head of Bank of America's Global Wealth business. Admiringly, Sallie has since launched a digital investment platform specifically for women aimed at closing the gender investing gap in the US.

I've also had many inspiring mentors who have influenced and guided me throughout my career. I cannot stress enough the importance of having mentors who can offer guidance, support, and invaluable insights as you navigate your personal and professional journey.

GOALS AND PURPOSE

Financial security is so important for us all, especially for women. By instilling sound financial habits, educating people about the importance of investing, and promoting financial literacy, I play a role in empowering individuals to make better, more informed decisions about their money.

I'm also committed to empowering women; I want to ensure that they feel confident to be heard, be brave in their careers, make choices that provide opportunities and put their hands up for promotion.

I would love to see more senior female leaders in the banking and finance industry. Women are seriously under-represented in the C-Suite. By harnessing the talents and perspectives of women, and increasing their representation in senior leadership roles, organisations are enriched.

"Without gender balance, we end up flying on one wing" (Katherine Zappone, former Minister for Children and Youth Affairs in Ireland).

FUTURE ASPIRATIONS

As my career has evolved, there have been other defining moments. Most of these are anchored in having strong mentors and sponsors. Moving into private banking and wealth management, I was lucky enough to have an incredible female mentor who believed in my talents, gave me outstanding advice, coached me, and inspired me to take on bigger and more important roles.

My advice to anyone looking to succeed is to find brilliant mentors who you admire and who are willing to invest in you professionally and personally, and to find senior sponsors who can leverage their networks and be your career champions.

PIA'S ADVICE

- *Don't be afraid to 'dream big'. If an opportunity comes your way that you don't feel you're quite ready for, or is outside your comfort zone, say yes. Step up and bridge the confidence gap. More often than not you'll learn quickly and grow immensely from the experience. Trust in your ability to rise to the occasion.*

- *Seek out mentors and sponsors throughout your career to guide, coach and champion your career journey. And pay it forward – be a mentor to others.*

- *Always be kind and show empathy. EQ (emotional intelligence) is as important, if not more important, than IQ. "No act of kindness, no matter how small, is ever wasted" (Aesop).*

- *Focus on growing your network. A robust network increases your visibility, provides greater access to career opportunities, can help with knowledge sharing and learning and is a valuable source of support and guidance.*

CHRISTINA MANTOURA GOUGH

BUSINESS WOMAN AND FOUNDER OF THE HOT TUB & SWIM SPA COMPANY

A successful woman in the spa and wellness industry, Christina Mantoura Gough has made an incredible impact. Christina sits on several industry panels and is regularly interviewed as a wellness, hot tub and spa expert. Her motto is "everyday happiness".

My sociable and sparkly personality meant I never blended into the background. I am sporty, and I've always pushed myself to achieve. I have modelled and travelled extensively, and I've competed in the national championships for athletics, karate and basketball. I therefore understand the importance of consistency and commitment. This attitude has definitely filtered through to my professional life. I have always striven to be exceptional, and I found my niche in the spas, hot tubs and wellness world. My parents instilled superb ethics in me, as well as the importance of resilience.

My mum was a world record holder, Commonwealth Games gold medallist, Olympic swimmer and a Speedo model. She started my passion for this industry. My dad was also sporty: a national basketball finalist, a black belt in karate and a scratch golfer! You have to have drive and inner strength to be successful and to continue even when facing obstacles. Being passionate and knowing your "reason" is so important. What's equally important to me is to surround yourself with superb people with similar values as no hand claps on its own. My darling dad taught me, "It's tough at the top," and I've never forgotten that. Being respectful and genuine, both professionally and personally, are values of mine, and I love to learn from people. Family is very important to me. I taught myself to always be positive. I wholeheartedly believe that the path of life is exciting if you have the right attitude.

BUILDING MY CAREER

I took a Management and Business Administration degree at university with extra language modules as I knew I wanted to get into international business. After sitting on the University Senate and being voted Best Management Student, I left and went into the banking sector. I was offered a graduate scheme at the leading management consultants in London, which was more in tune with my personality. Whilst waiting for the role to start I could be found tanning around my parent's swimming pool in what was the hottest summer on British record! They ran a swimming pool and hot tub showroom and asked whether I could help support them for a few weeks selling chlorine through the heatwave. I responded, "Gladly… but only if I can wear shorts!" And there ended my City days wearing power suits and started my incredible career, initially in my family business and then, in 2015, founding my own company.

One of my pivotal moments after working with my parents for a few weeks was selling a gentleman our flagship spa hot tub, and he happily gave me a £3,000 deposit even though I wouldn't know the price until the following day! I have always been extremely enthusiastic about high-quality and technology-led hydrotherapy spas, and I think that resonates with people. The next day, the customer laughed, agreed (of course) and insisted I must go and work for him due to my passion and, I suppose, intrinsic confidence. I politely declined as I knew then if I were to be good at something, I'd want to earn money for my family and not for others.

Family businesses can be very emotionally rewarding, too, if you work with the right people. I was earning half of what I would be on the London graduate scheme, but somehow, at that time, that didn't matter, as I saw the bigger picture and we were having fun! From there, I set about learning everything I could about the industry, products, how we could differentiate ourselves, and most importantly, how we could be consistently better than the rest.

THE INSPIRATION

Wellness is a fast-evolving industry, and you have to stay ahead. I travelled the world for training and attended most high-profile trade shows. People working on their well-being inspire me. I am interested in constant improvement and biohacking, so I listen to a lot of audiobooks on the power of the mind and unique people. I take snippets from each and form my own opinions. I learnt a lot from my dad, who still remains the most refined salesperson. I have an epic team who believe in our culture, and that's another reason we win so many awards. My core values are to be a knowledge geek, to trust your products, to know your customers and to be more polished than the rest! Trends come and go, but I am focused on our industry growing using incredible technological advances and effective, sustainable solutions. People have always loved hydrotherapy spas and heat treatments, such as saunas and steams, but infrared and cold treatments, such as very cold spas or ice treatments, are rising in popularity.

We support numerous charities, but those that sit closest to my heart are children's charities and water aid charities, although we contribute to numerous others, including supporting start-up businesses in war-torn counties. We have made a few, very special children happy over the years with spas for palliative care. Life is precious.

CHALLENGES

The early days of my career were fun. We quickly became one of the largest hot tub retailers in Europe. We were invited to become UK importers and distributors of a high-quality hot tub manufacturer based in Canada, known for their outstanding product. They were selling, and we were growing, opening new showrooms as a result. One day, quite early into the recession, the manufacturer stopped picking up the phone and responding to emails. They'd gone into liquidation without telling us, leaving us with over 120 hot tubs in inventory in the UK suddenly with no manufacturer warranty.

This left us totally alone to service and support our customers and our dealers. This was a huge blow financially and emotionally. The recession really took its toll on the luxury and spa industry and took out some very big players. How did we get through? We didn't give up; we kept smiling, even though it was very hard, and we made some tough choices. We reduced the number of our showrooms and shrunk our team down to core team members. We kept those who had the right attitude, and together, we focused on unparalleled customer care and our marketing mix.

When I started my own firm, I diversified into self-cleaning swim spas, an incredible product and one of the fastest-growing pool solutions worldwide! It complemented our self-cleaning hot tubs beautifully. I knew it was important to have an exceptional product portfolio, with the key products in conjunction with innovative ones that offer a creative edge. I loathe a loss leader so I focus on stocking lines that move quickly, but I know the added value of having bespoke and custom items.

TO BECOME A SUCCESS

Self-care isn't a nice-to-do anymore; it's a must-do.

People understand the dangers of working with stress, poor nutrition, lack of exercise and insufficient quality sleep. People are spending more time and money on investing in themselves. You must look after yourself mentally and physically first, as, without one or both, everything falls apart.

We should consider our body like the only home we truly own! Hydrotherapy, saunas, cold therapy, hot tubs and infra really help keep people healthy and their mind-sets elevated.

Ensure you dare to dream big and grasp opportunities, but be prepared to put in consistent effort. My mindset believes less in luck and more in perseverance, meaning you will gradually become better and more fortunate.

I surround myself with people who work their socks off to achieve gradual steps to greatness, but I also follow my gut instincts. Improving one hundred things by 1% each starts turning dreams into a reality.

I think I have a knack for spotting a product opportunity – the rise of the swim spa, appropriate stock levels through testing times like COVID-19, and engaging in new products so we have a first-mover advantage. Our firm even won an innovation award. It is the most exciting industry to be a leader in, as people love the products.

CAREER SUCCESS

I didn't want an ordinary life, so I worked hard to create an exceptional one. I was chosen to design and install the largest number of exclusive residential hot tubs for iconic apartment blocks in Central London overlooking the River Thames. In the last six years, I have been the most interviewed lady in this field on national and international TV and radio, plus written press, including newspapers. I loved being featured in the *Sunday Times*, and it was written that we are the only luxury hot tub retailer of choice, highlighting the outstanding service my team provides. We now have the largest number of positive reviews of any UK spa and wellness company.

Our company slogan came from friends who regularly tell me I am one of the happiest people they know, so that was it. "Everyday Happiness" was born, as that's what our products do – they make people happy!

CHRISTINA'S TIPS

- *Take your well-being and wellness seriously and invest in it.*

- *Be focused and resilient in equal measure.*

- *Strive for excellence, prioritise and don't tolerate sub-standard.*

- *There is power in a beautiful showroom and excellent calibre people.*

- *Be unique. People will copy you when things are going well, and that's flattering. That's why you must never stop trying to be better and must provide outstanding customer care as a business.*

- *Be a champion of other women and family businesses.*

DON'T WORRY ABOUT BEING SUCCESSFUL BUT WORK TOWARD BEING SIGNIFICANT AND THE SUCCESS WILL NATURALLY FOLLOW.

OPRAH WINFREY

EMMA JANE PILKINGTON

INTERIOR DESIGNER

Emma Jane Pilkington is an internationally recognised tastemaker and interior designer. Emma's polished yet eclectic style has been celebrated in publications such as ELLE Decor *(A-List),* House and Garden, The *New York Times and* Vogue, *to name a few. Based in Greenwich, Connecticut, she is called upon by clients across the world for her sharp eye and impeccable taste.*

I never planned to be an interior designer. Ever since I can remember, I always wanted to be a fashion designer. In Australia, as a little girl, I would devour American and French *Vogue* and obsess about what to wear on the one 'free' day of the year when we were not required to wear our strict English school uniforms – wool Black Watch tartan in the sweltering Sydney heat!

After college, I interned for the American couturier, James Purcell, on Seventh Avenue in New York. I had spent the previous summer at Parsons (fashion school) and I assisted a stylist, working backstage at some great shows. It was the era of Kate Moss, Marc Jacobs and grunge. I loved it all. I have always had a strong interior dialogue in regard to aesthetics. It is my perpetual visual escapism. I moved on to fashion editorials, until an illness sidetracked me. It was then that I fell into Interiors.

I remember the day; it had started so well. It was August, and I was on the beach in the Hamptons when my sister called. She told me that she had recommended me for an interior design job in Manhattan. My heart skipped in one of those moments when you know that your life is about to change. I was hired; shortly afterwards, the contractor left, and I had to learn on my feet. I spent all my free time visiting showrooms, antique stores and fabric houses, poring over interior design books – I could not get enough. When you bounce out of bed with excitement, you must be on the right course.

In the beginning, I read and re-read Rose Tarlow's book *The Private House* as well as the Hunniford Sills book, *Dwellings*. There was an attitude and an intimacy in them that hooked me. I responded to the light, the juxtaposition of the old and the new, and the subtle hand of a fabric. I wanted to live in these rooms. I wanted to create those rooms! As I studied historical periods at night and worked with top artisans during the day, I also honed my instinctual sense of space and scale. Seeing a project come together was exciting. I derived great pleasure from the smallest detail. With my innate ability to read a space and to envision how to furnish it, I realised that a career in the field could actually be fun!

The flipside to being creative can be the human element. I am by nature an introvert and, as such, I find strength in solitude. In the beginning, I found learning how to navigate the client relationship to be rewarding and inspiring, but at times, it could be taxing. I lived and breathed a project, and with excitement also comes disillusion. I taught myself to be more detached, and this has served me well.

BUILDING SUCCESS

My interiors are not scripted; rather, they come from the gut. Perhaps my work has been successful because people respond as they would to a sincere conversation. I personally design each project so there is never repetition. I made the decision to keep my business small so I could continue to work in this manner. I need to be able to completely submerge myself in a place. Sort of like an actor living a role. I am also proud and honoured to have been recognised within the industry. It still thrills me to be included in certain company, on various lists. A legendary talent once wrote me a note congratulating me on my work, and I have kept it close to my desk ever since.

When I started my business, success was supported through editorials. Today, success is linked implicitly to social media. Being a private person, to date I have resisted the call. I am tempted, but it is a Pandora's box that I am still hesitant to open. I have enjoyed an organic success in both media and I have been fortunate to have done so without the need for self-promotion.

INSPIRATIONS

My first mentor was my mother. Wherever we moved in the world, she had an amazing ability to create a beautiful home. Her rooms are just perfect. She has been my design partner and backbone from the beginning. We started working together when she moved to New York. We share a similar aesthetic, and I can trust her responses implicitly. We also have great fun! I adore our days working together.

One of my earliest champions was Cynthia Frank. Larger than life, Cynthia was then an editor at *House and Garden* (how I miss that magazine!), and she introduced me to Dominique Browning, the editor-in-chief. Between wonderful editorial coverage and inclusion in the inaugural Tastemaker List, they really helped to launch my career. For that, I am eternally grateful.

The most exciting people I've worked with were actually a team of brilliant designers and producers. I was asked to design the Moët and Chandon marquee at the Melbourne Cup. It was to be based on the Hall of Mirrors at Versailles. I worked remotely from the States with an incredible team in Melbourne. When I arrived there, the marquee was even more perfect than I could have imagined. I was born in Melbourne, and the welcome that I received was very touching. This was a particularly exciting project for me.

Throughout my career, I have certainly had projects that get cut short or clients that disappoint me. Fortunately, another opportunity always comes along and my energy gets restored.

EMMA'S TIPS

- *Identify your passion, feed it and commit to it 100%.*

- *Do not take a break until the foundation is strong.*

- *Learn from others and be humble.*

SAMANTHA WILLS

JEWELLERY ENTREPRENEUR AND FOUNDER OF THE SAMANTHA WILLS FOUNDATION

A celebrated entrepreneur, Samantha Wills has built one of the best-known accessories brands. Her desire to support emerging founders saw her create the Samantha Wills Foundation in 2016, a platform designed to empower women in business.

I am an only child, so I found ways to be creative to occupy myself. I was always moving my room around. Every single week I would do a mini-renovation in there. Mum and Dad gave me full creative freedom for my bedroom, so I had the walls painted different colours, fairy lights strewn everywhere. Once I even took the doors off the wardrobe and had the bed coming out of it so it was like a canopy. I am surprised I didn't go into interior design!

But everything I did was creative: being creative is where I felt most myself. When I was 11 years old, my mum put me into a beading class at a local craft store. She was probably doing it to keep me out of her hair in the school holidays, but what my mum really gave me was the foundation on which my career was built. I learnt the basics of jewellery-making in those classes.

STARTING OUT

Mum and Dad always had small businesses. In 1993 they opened a clothing boutique, and my mum let me have a tiny space on the counter to sell jewellery. I was selling about $50 worth a week, and I was 12 years old. I barely finished high school and did not go to university. When I finished high school (1999), the internet was not nearly as accessible or prevalent as it is now. I grew up in small-town Port Macquarie in Australia and didn't know that being a creative director was actually a career choice. I thought I was just destined to get a 'job' and then do my creative pursuits as hobbies on the side.

I moved to Sydney when I was 20 years old and started making jewellery in the evenings just for fun while working a retail job during the day. Friends came over and bought a few pieces, then they asked me to go to their house with the jewellery so they could invite their friends over. This little organic jewellery party-type business started! I then started selling down at Bondi Markets every Sunday and was offered a spot on a showroom wall at fashion week in 2004.

I had just turned 22 years old. I took the spot (which cost $500 – I had $509 in the bank at the time!) and hoped to make one order back. I ended up writing $17,000 worth of orders in the four days of Fashion Week. So I quit my 'job' the next day and gave everything I had emotionally, financially and spiritually to building the Samantha Wills jewellery business.

EXPANDING THE BRAND
After Fashion Week, my entire perspective on my business changed. Before Fashion Week, the jewellery making was just a side hobby. The interest I got from retailers at Fashion Week was also like permission or validation that I had a viable business concept. I hit the ground running, and over the following three years I did everything myself, from manufacturing the product to selling, shipping, invoicing, designing … all of it. What became very evident was that I knew how to build a brand but not how to run a business. I got myself into $80,000 worth of debt.

I was at the end of the line. I couldn't borrow any more money and was about to sign 51% of the company over to an investor just to be saved from bankruptcy. But in the wonderful way the universe works, I met my now business partner the same week I was about the sign the contract. I convinced him to join me in the business, and without putting a cent in, he turned the debt around in six months. With his commercial mind and my creative mind, we had the perfect partnership to build a very creative brand with a very commercial business structure.

Meeting my business partner three years in brought a calmness to the business and allowed me to focus on what I am good at – building the brand. When I was able to do that with support and infrastructure around me, the brand and business took off in a huge way. Having the systems and processes in place meant we were ready for high growth.

SOCIAL MEDIA HAS A LOT TO ANSWER FOR
I think the tech giants have a lot to answer for. The way we are addicted to social media is not dissimilar to the addiction to slot machines. I think the recent implementation of removing 'likes' is very important and a great step towards supporting mental health, but social media is a very slippery slope on many levels, from the 'compare and despair' that I know is prevalent, especially in females, to the false ads that were created and targeted in the US 2016 election. There has to be a responsibility of truth, both from users and facilitators.

THE CHALLENGES
One of the biggest challenges for me was a relationship break-up. While my career publicly was going from strength to strength, my personal life was in destruction. I was barely able to function and spent a lot of time on the floor of hotel bathrooms trying to just breathe. I would set my alarm for an hour earlier then I knew I had to be at my first engagement for the day just so I knew I had an hour scheduled to fall apart before I had to step into a very public role. And I think that is one of the things in business or entrepreneurship –the world doesn't stop when we are grieving. The show must go on, and if it's your business there is no option of calling in sick to the boss, because you are the boss. This challenge taught me so much about what I would tolerate, about resistance, about alchemy and about being truthful with myself.

From every challenge there is a purpose, and I held on so tightly to things that were not serving me and I sat in the darkness of that for a long time. When I finally started to rebuild, I emerged with a greater purpose from it, and my alchemy out of it was launching the Samantha Wills Foundation: a platform created to empower women in business. I knew that if I had experienced what I just had, that others might have also and I felt it important to share the vulnerabilities of what it takes to run a business, especially when things may be on the verge of turmoil in your private life. I believe that sharing our vulnerabilities is such an important part of empowering others. That is where we find connection, when we can see ourselves in another's story.

MY INSPIRATIONS
BRAND: When I started the Samantha Wills brand, I was so inspired by what Jodhi Meares had built with Tigerlily. It was one of the first lifestyle brands I really admired – they invited you beyond the product.

BUSINESS: My business partner Geoff Bainbridge has been a long-time inspiration to me. We have not always seen eye to eye, but I have learnt so much about how business and brand meet and co-exist from him.

VALUES: I am a huge admirer of Taylor Swift – the way she remains steadfast to her values and uses her position and platform to fight the fight, knowing it will help others who are following in her path, is amazing.

BEING A POWERHOUSE IS….
Someone who empowers others. They make others feel seen and validated.

SAMANTHA'S MOTTO
The Universe only ever has three answers for us: Yes. Not right now. I have something better in store for you.

SAMANTHA'S TIPS

- *Purpose: Know your why. Business is what we do, but brand is why we do it. You will stray from your why often, but it is imperative that you know it clearly so that you can return to it always.*

- *Intuition: Invest in understanding your intuition. How does your intuition communicate with you? Take time and create space to develop this; it is an incredibly powerful tool for business.*

- *Surrender: Surrendering is very different to giving up. Surrender is looking around at the lesson you are trying to be shown when you hit a roadblock or closed door. Surrendering is keeping an open mind and perspective. It is listening to your intuition and hearing where you are being guided to go. When we truly surrender, we see things differently; we note the coincidences that are playing out around us and we allow our intuition to have a voice.*

JESS SEPEL

BESTSELLING AUTHOR AND NUTRITIONIST

Jessica's approach to a healthy lifestyle is informed by a well-researched understanding of nutrition and complemented by a passion to achieve physical and psychological balance. Her approach to health and nutrition aims to inspire people to live the best possible lifestyle by maintaining a healthy relationship with food and themselves.

I was in a bit of a slump before I started. I wasn't exactly living the best life. I was partying too much, waking up incredibly anxious, a chronic fad dieter and buried in low self-esteem. Life didn't feel so good. I was very disconnected to my own body.

I studied health and nutrition for five years, and learning about the body in such an in-depth way was my trigger to change. I was starting to understand that I wasn't treating my body very well. I started making healthier choices and created space for balance in my life – and my body (and life) started healing. I created a blog to write about how I was healing and the healthy recipes I was discovering. My intention was to help as many women as I could, who were going through the same struggles as I was.

At the beginning, the biggest challenge was feeling worthy of the success of the blog. The blog became popular quite quickly, and something I find challenging is overcoming self-doubt – I am working on it! Nowadays, I feel success is waking up every day, feeling fulfilled in my personal and business life. Waking up and being able to look forward to my day – this has got to be the new definition of success!

THE HEALTHY LIFE

I think the biggest challenge has been healing myself and turning my life into something I love. I also feel so proud of all the people who have come along with me on my journey and embraced the healthy life; it is an achievement that I share with my community.

Nowadays, I am continually inspired by my community and patients from my nutrition clinic. I am constantly inspired by their desire to change/heal and embrace a healthier life. Their progress is incredibly inspiring. My mum has always been the best healthy cook I know. She taught me what it means to eat real wholefoods. My grandmother is

also an incredible health role model who has always inspired me with her healthy way of life.

THE JS HEALTH COMMUNITY

I am very in touch with my community – I listen to them. I watch their comments on social media and read all the emails I receive to make sure the advice and recipes I put out to them are in response to what they're needing. For example, I will receive an email from someone asking for more main meal ideas – and then I will know to create more main meals on the blog. It has been a challenge to stay honest, because being honest means you're open and vulnerable.

I started the blog as an outlet to keep a record of my own health journey as I studied nutrition, but I ever expected it to become what it has today – so that's why it's so important, but sometimes a little difficult, to keep it so personal. Sometimes, I can be my own setback – I can be incredibly hard on myself. Being a perfectionist is a disadvantage at times. It makes you feel you are not doing enough. Acknowledging all that I have done and created helps me overcome that.

JESS'S TIPS

- *Be authentic, be real – being real is relatable. If you are an aspiring blogger – have a powerful message that you know will resonate. Don't be afraid to share your story.*

- *Focus on your work – not others'. Keep your eye on your stuff. Don't compare yourself: it is a waste of time. That is a setback.*

- *Dream big. No more limits. Know you are worthy of success. I talk a lot about this in my books and blogs. You have to work on knowing your worth and believing you are deserving of success.*

*SOME WOMEN
FEAR THE FIRE.
SOME ACTUALLY
BECOME IT.*

R.H.SIN

ELIZABETH DART

ENTREPRENEUR, FOUNDER OF HUNTER & QUEEN

Elizabeth Dart is the founder of Hunter & Queen, a luxury lifestyle brand grounded in timeless design, resilience, and purpose. The brand name was inspired by "Elizabeth Hunter," a name she once carried and now reclaims as a legacy for her children – a symbol of grace for all ages.

From a young age, I was drawn to beauty, self-expression, and creating something lasting. I was the girl redesigning Barbie's outfits, obsessed with fabrics, fashion, and storytelling through style. I got my first job at thirteen on my father's golf course, then worked at Country Road, spending every cent on new-season trends.

I grew up in a home filled with warmth, curiosity, and contrast – where one parent taught me elegance, and the other taught me to shoot clay targets and reverse park a manual car by twelve. I learned kindness from my mother and tenacity from my father. We travelled often, and at twelve, I fell in love with Hong Kong – a city I would call home three separate times across my life.

My teenage years included competitive ice skating, netball, tennis, and days running into the surf. I stepped into modelling at fifteen, eventually doing a small stint in television for C7 Sport in NSW before moving to New York at the age of twenty-six, with a six-month-old son and my first husband who remains a close friend to this day. But life wasn't without its shadows – self-doubt, heartbreak, and eventually living through financial, physical and emotional abuse would shape the years to come when I re-married. Still, I've always loved love, always dreamed of a big family, and always put my children first. I've never stopped chasing the dream that one day, it would all mean something. I was judged by on lookers, without many wanting to know the truth. Domestic violence is still a challenge for the victim not the perpetrators when it comes to public perception, gossip and further trauma by perpetrators family and friends gathering numbers trying to destroy the reputation to save their family members.

THE BEGINNING OF HUNTER & QUEEN

Hunter & Queen was born from both necessity and vision. After leaving a long-term abusive marriage, I needed to create something of my own – something lasting and meaningful. The brand concept lingered in my mind for years, but it was during COVID lockdown, while homeschooling in my apartment, that I finally gave it life.

We launched with a single signature product – the Travel Rug – designed to be beautiful, durable, and versatile. It marked my return to the world as a founder. In 2025, an investor came on board who believed in both the brand and my leadership. Today, Hunter & Queen is expanding into resort wear, swim, and curated accessories. Over the next 5–10 years, I envision the brand scaling internationally through retail partnerships, resort collaborations, and immersive consumer experiences.

CREATIVE PROCESS

My design aesthetic balances opposing forces – utility with elegance, softness with structure. I'm inspired by the European summer lifestyle, grounded by the rawness of the Australian coastline.

The Hunter & Queen crest is a prominent feature in our outdoor range, while our resort collections speak more subtly through form and fabric. We are currently stocked in select boutiques across

Australia and New Zealand, with plans underway for global retail rollout.

We began intentionally with outdoor accessories – a way to test systems, logistics, and grow community through honest storytelling with social media and slow fashion values.

LONG TERM SUCCESS
Discipline, courage, clarity, and consistency. Success isn't simply about talent – it's about execution. It takes hard work, many late nights, and a can-do attitude no matter how tired you are. You must also cultivate resilience, emotional intelligence, and the humility to keep learning.

OVERCOMING CHALLENGES
Years ago, I pursued an opportunity involving a Hydration Wellness Drink with global potential. I relocated to Hong Kong with my daughters, while my son remained in senior boarding school. Unfortunately, the business partnership collapsed, a school placement for one daughter fell through, and I was left emotionally and financially vulnerable.

This wasn't about ego – it was about survival. I needed to build independence so I could exit a volatile marriage and protect my family. Divorce proceedings began with borrowed funds, and I faced a significant reputational battle as misinformation was spread. My father had always advised me: document everything. That advice proved crucial.

I rebuilt from the ground up. Quietly. Intentionally. With every setback, I refocused on the future I was determined to create.

LEADING THROUGH OBSTACLES
Not everyone will understand your vision – and that's okay. Doubt from others can be fuel if you allow it. It's also taught me to identify self-sabotage early and recalibrate fast. The path to building a brand isn't linear – and most of the important wins happen without an audience.

CAREER CHALLENGES
Balancing entrepreneurship with parenting, navigating the emotional toll of DV recovery, securing capital without traditional backing, and reestablishing a professional reputation after years of personal attacks.

GREATEST INFLUENCES
My children for their ability to adapt under extraordinary circumstances and seek new memories with great purpose. My father, who is tenacious and loyal. My mother, who is graceful, empathetic, and always puts others first. My sister, who is quiet yet protective, in a a real-life Beth Dutton style. And two school friends, whose belief in me changed everything. In the public space, women like Diane von Furstenberg have inspired me for turning heartbreak into heritage.

CAREER MILESTONES
In my twenties, I started a maternity brand, Precious Cargo. It did well, but I sold out early to support my then-husband's real estate career. We used over $250k of my savings to move to Singapore and give him a head start. His career soared, and though it wasn't my dream, I'm proud of that chapter. Now, I'm focused on building Hunter & Queen into a global brand that can stand beside the best – not in their shadow, but on its own terms.

STARTING METTLE BEE
Mettle Bee is a fintech safety platform designed to support women escaping domestic violence. It offers discreet financial tools, encrypted safety features, and access to emergency resources – empowering women to plan safe departures with autonomy and confidence.

The platform was recently sold to an undisclosed U.S.-based buyer focused on ethical and impact-driven technology. While the terms of the acquisition remain confidential, I will continue in an advisory capacity to guide its global rollout over the next 12 months.

Mettle Bee stands as proof that survivor-led innovation isn't just vital – it's powerful, scalable, and worth investing in.

INTERNATIONAL PROJECTS
We're working on a Hunter & Queen fragrance and quietly building a foundation to help women rebuild their lives and launch businesses of their own through my advocacy work. I am involved in advocacy work for Rize Up Australia and other DV services.

CAREER ADVICE

Don't wait to be discovered. Build yourself into someone who cannot be ignored. Back yourself harder than anyone else will. Know your numbers. Protect your ideas. Don't flinch when they try to shake you – they only do it when they feel your power of energy.

A POWERHOUSE

A powerhouse is someone who leads with empathy, holds firm in chaos, and uses her story to drive systemic impact. She is grounded, focused, and unwilling to let adversity steal her light.

LIZ'S ADVICE

- *Build yourself into someone who cannot be ignored.*

- *Back yourself harder than anyone else will.*

- *Protect your ideas.*

- *Don't flinch when they try to shake you – they only do it when they feel your power of energy.*

- *Don't wait to be discovered.*

BOBBI BROWN

MAKEUP ARTIST AND FOUNDER OF BOBBI BROWN COSMETICS

Bobbi Brown is the name and brains behind one of the top cosmetic brands in the world. As a makeup artist she started with a simple idea, and her brand is now sold in more than 70 countries worldwide. She is a champion for women's rights and passionate about female empowerment through education. She volunteers for a number of charities and believes strongly in giving back.

Makeup has always been my passion – it started when I was five years old and got into my mother's makeup drawer – I began playing with her makeup, applying it to my face, the sink and even the bathroom walls. As I grew up, I still loved playing with makeup and my parents encouraged me to 'go for it'.

One winter, while home from college, I told my mother that I wanted to drop out of school. She said I couldn't and insisted that I get a college degree – and I thank her for it. She asked me what I wanted to do when I finished school and I had no idea. Then she said something that is so simple, but changed my life. She said, "Forget about what you want to do with your life – pretend it's your birthday and you can do anything you want." I stopped and said I wanted to go to Marshall Fields (a Chicago department store) and play with makeup. And she said, "Why don't you study cosmetics and get a degree from a school somewhere?" My passion for makeup led me to Emerson College in Boston, where I pursued a degree in theatrical makeup.

After graduating from college, I headed to New York to fulfil my dream of working as a professional makeup artist. It was the 1980s, and the look of the moment was loud, garish and overdone. I soon became frustrated by the lack of flattering makeup on the market. It was impossible to find makeup that looked good on the skin. I almost always had to mix the products I bought, blending shades together until I got something that looked natural. I saw a major void in the cosmetics industry that I knew I could help address. My vision was to create a cosmetics line that looked natural and would match and complement women's complexions. I started with creating lipstick shades that made lips look like lips, only better.

I had an idea to develop a flattering lipstick – something that was different from everything available in stores. I realised that not everybody loved neutrals, so I thought about 10 different women I knew and what colours would look good on them. With this set of ten lipsticks, a woman could create an infinite number of wearable shades just by mixing and blending them. After launching my original 10 lipsticks at Bergdorf Goodman in February 1991, I knew a beauty revolution was underway. Women really embraced these uniquely flattering shades and my realistic approach to beauty.

The launch of Bobbi Brown Essentials at Bergdorf Goodman in 1991 was an iconic moment for me, and I remember it like it was yesterday. I thought we would sell 100 lipsticks in the first month, and we sold 100 in the first day.

BOBBI'S TIPS

- *You need a unique idea, you need to be passionate about your craft, and you have to work hard.*

- *Don't stop at the first hurdle that you meet. You must keep your goal in mind and move forward.*

- *And most important, you need to trust your instincts.*

TAMARA RALPH

CREATIVE DIRECTOR AND CO-FOUNDER OF RALPH & RUSSO

Tamara Ralph became the first female Creative Director from the UK in nearly 100 years to be deemed eligible to show during Paris Haute Couture Week. International fashion label Ralph & Russo is beloved by women worldwide.

I was born into a creative family with four generations of couturiers, so fashion and design have always been a part of my life and have been passions I explored from an early age. I started amending my mother's clothes at the age of 12, much to her surprise!

I always knew growing up that I wanted to be a fashion designer. My parents often joke that before I'd even become a teenager, I'd mentioned having my own brand one day and had planned it all out in my head. I've been lucky, really, to have that calling from such a young age because it's informed me in every stage of my life as to the end goal.

THE MAKING OF RALPH & RUSSO

I started creating bespoke gowns when I was at school. I had a dear friend who saw the pieces I had made and asked if I could make her one, so I said, "Of course, darling... but you'll have to pay!" This is how I secured my very first client.

I'd always had this dream of creating a luxury lifestyle brand, and upon meeting Michael (Russo), who also shared the same vision, we were set to get to work, as they say. Initially, we decided to launch as a couture brand. With my background servicing private clients with bespoke pieces, and with there being such a gap in the market at the time for couture, we felt that playing to our strengths in this sense was the best possible business plan, and that was essentially how we got Ralph & Russo off the ground.

EXPANDING THE BRAND

I think especially when we were starting out and with much of our brand awareness having been garnered through word of mouth, having high-profile clients like HRH Sheikha Moza and Angelina Jolie call us to place orders were incredible moments of realisation for us and act as a testament to the brand taking off. Additionally, being invited to show on the official Paris Haute Couture Week schedule by the Chambre Syndicale de la Haute Couture was a pivotal moment for us. It put the brand on the map in terms of receiving recognition on a global scale and aligning us alongside the likes of the powerhouses of Chanel, Dior and Valentino.

THE CHALLENGES

Launching a business outside of Australia was and remains a huge challenge, especially in today's modern and constantly evolving climate, but as a designer you naturally have a mindset of believing that truly anything is possible.

I think two key challenges that are affecting designers across the board are the preservation of age-old artisanal techniques and sustainability. On both counts, we have a responsibility to the industry and to our planet to strike a balance and ensure that both are being nurtured in tandem.

Launching a brand is no easy feat, and I think that, often, people can be quick to put you in a box: to judge, to define your skill set or capability, without knowing who you really are. I think from all the challenges I've faced, I've really come to understand the importance of self-belief and of grit. You have to remind yourself along the way that you have what it takes to go far and never to give in – as one of the great orators of the world once said, "Wars are not won by evacuation," and neither are challenges.

THE INSPIRATION

As a designer, I'm constantly inspired by everything around me, be it from something I've heard in conversation, a book I'm reading, an exhibition I've just seen or an experience: it can be from the simplest thing. I always find travelling and understanding new cultures incredibly inspiring. As a creative, you must constantly have an open mind and be receptive to new ideas or waves of inspiration, and travel really gratifies that: it allows you to immerse yourself completely in another world.

The world, to the eye of a creative, really is a lens of opportunity. It can be so inspiring that sometimes it's a bit like having a lightbulb moment but without the switch off!

FEMALE EMPOWERMENT

There's no doubt about it, it's an incredible movement and one that I wholeheartedly support. It's been so wonderfully inspiring seeing women come together across the globe and in all industries – be it for the #MeToo movement or fighting for the female right to drive in Saudi Arabia – women are finally claiming their voice and standing up for the rights of future generations.

BEING A POWERHOUSE

To be a Powerhouse is to be an innovator. To trust your own vision and empower yourself to move forward in a way that may be new or challenging, even controversial: to change the game by changing the rules.

MY MOTTO

"Exercise graciousness and humility in all that you do. Dream big, and never give up."

TAMARA'S TIPS

- *As an entrepreneur, you're constantly learning, and I would be lying to you if I said that every business worked in the same way. I think the best advice for anyone looking to succeed in business is to pursue a career you are passionate about, be prepared to work incredibly hard and don't sweat the small stuff.*

- *Success is an uphill struggle, but hard work always pays off in the end.*

DR BARBARA STURM

SKINCARE ENTREPRENEUR

Dr Barbara Sturm started her career as a surgeon, developing treatments for her patients using their own proteins. Research led her to adopt these same principles and apply them to skin care. She launched her eponymous line in 2014.

I was a tomboy and loved spending my childhood outside in nature. In the winter months, my grandmother, who was a pharmacist, would make us a rich and protective cream. We grew up in Germany in the mountains and had snow every winter. My mum, who was a chemist and lab doctor, loved milk baths and dry brushing and would always mix creams for us as children. We would often go into the forest during my childhood and pick medicinal herbs and roots. So, even as a kid, I was interested in both chemistry and pharmacy, and that led me in the direction of medicine.

STARTING OUT

I began my medical career in anti-inflammatory-focused orthopaedic medicine. I translated some of our early, innovative research directed towards arthritic joints into the skin in 2002. My passion and inspiration come from my mother, who was a pharmacist, and my grandmother, who was also a pharmacist. My products are always first inspired by and designed for my family and friends before I offer them to the public. My Baby & Kids line is one example – I created these formulations for my youngest daughter, Pepper, and she was their only customer for the first year. I made more in the lab for friends, and eventually, I decided to offer it to the public. I began developing my Dr Barbara Sturm Molecular Cosmetics line with a single, bespoke, patients-only cream called 'MC1'. My patients ultimately asked me what they should use as an overall skincare regimen, and I set out to formulate my own, as I could not recommend anything on the market. It took me several years, but the result was Molecular Cosmetics, an entirely science-driven, high-performance skincare regimen. The stars of my products are the ingredients and the science that underpins them, which combine in formulation medleys that create beautiful, healthy skin.

THE TIPPING POINT: THE VAMPIRE FACIAL
Fifteen years ago, I invented a treatment using patients' own blood proteins.

Although I did not name it, the treatment was later termed the 'vampire facial' by the public. This treatment harnesses the strong anti-inflammatory, regenerative and healing properties of the body's own proteins. These natural proteins are amplified 140 times using a special technique and can then be re-injected into the skin, mixed with hyaluronic fillers or added to my bespoke 'MC1' face cream, which also became a cult product.

THE CHALLENGES
Beauty and wellness represent a huge, competitive industry and like a lot of industries, it doesn't like the changes it is facing to its old status quo. I have been outspoken about the approaches that I believe are good and bad for your skin, not just about my own products. You know you have come to the attention of many large competitors in your industry when they start to attack you.

I faced challenges when I started out that I don't have now. Some men are prone to telling women, "You can't do that," but certainly not all men. And by the way, some women are prone to telling you that too. It's just important for women to be confident and to have the courage of their convictions. Trust yourself.

OUR BRAND
Our brand is known to provide skincare solutions to everyone, especially those who have specific skin needs, such as the Clarifying line, Darker Skin Tone line, Brightening line and Mini Molecular Baby & Kids line. We have a solution for every skin tone and type, as well as targeted products for exfoliation, hydration, masking and to combat irritation. We are very established as a full beauty and skincare concept. That's my biggest success.

My products are like my children: I created each of them for a reason and don't pick favourites. But perhaps my most fundamental and most popular product is the HYALURONIC SERUM, which promotes skin barrier function and a healthy skin matrix and restores both superficial and deeper moisture reservoirs. I personally also couldn't live without my FACE MASK and wouldn't go out without my GLOW DROPS. Yet if I had to pick one product to survive, it would be my moisturising FACE CREAM.

MY SKIN TIPS
Firstly, I always make sure I have my supplements – diet and lifestyle are hard to keep controlled when travelling, which is when the supplements are super-important. I take my SKIN FOOD, REPAIR FOOD and ANTI-POLLUTION FOOD supplements every day with my breakfast, and if I'm jet-lagged I also take SLEEP FOOD before bed. Because I travel so much, I need to keep my skin care routine (and the products I tote around) minimalist. Travel presents unique skin inflammation triggers, with sleep deprivation, stress, changing climates, bacteria, and dry, cold air on the plane. My packing philosophy caters to these realities, and I have created travel-sized skincare products for this reason. Skin hydration and strengthening your skin barrier function are always important, but especially when we travel. I pack my CLEANSER, HYALURONIC SERUM, FACE CREAM and my FACE MASK, which is a real hero product when travelling. I bring my GLOW DROPS and wear that instead of makeup.

MY THOUGHTS ON SOCIAL MEDIA
My business would not have been possible without social media. It has levelled the playing field between innovative small start-ups and the goliaths in the skincare industry. Social media allows me to communicate directly with my customers to provide education and receive feedback.

WHAT IS A POWERHOUSE?
I think if you challenge the status quo and the conventional wisdom to create something new, you can be a Powerhouse.

MY ROLE MODELS
Two answers to this. First, my mother, who passed away eight years ago, inspires me in every way, and that inspiration comes to me from her every day. Professionally, I feel fortunate to have met and call friends some amazing entrepreneurial women. Anastasia Soare, Stella McCartney, Anita Ko and Jessica McCormack are each impressive in so many ways, but they all share these inspirational traits – total devotion to their customer and an insane work ethic.

MY MOTTO

I wish I could say I have one. But realistically I'm running out the door with a kid in one arm, work things in the other, and dozens of to-do's running through my mind. My mantra is to put one foot in front of the other, and keep moving.

BARBARA'S TIPS

- *Don't let anyone talk you out of your dream and vision.*

- *Focus on the passion, not the money.*

- *The customer is queen.*

- *Embrace and harness the disruptive changes of the internet and social media, which level the field. But the happy reality, and I see it every day, is that women entrepreneurism is exploding.*

> *THERE IS A POWERFUL DRIVING FORCE INSIDE EVERY HUMAN BEING THAT, ONCE UNLEASHED, CAN MAKE ANY VISION, DREAM OR DESIRE A REALITY.*

ANTHONY ROBBINS

YOUR NEXT LEVEL WON'T BE CHEERED IN. IT'LL BE CHALLENGED.
PEOPLE WILL DOUBT YOU.
SOME WILL LEAVE.
OTHERS WILL CRITICIZE WHAT THEY DON'T UNDERSTAND.
LET THEM.
YOU WEREN'T BUILT FOR APPROVAL.
YOU WERE BUILT FOR IMPACT.
BE UNSHAKABLE. BE LEGENDARY.
AND NEVER LOWER YOUR VISION TO MATCH SOMEONE ELSE'S COMFORT.

STEPH ADAMS
BESTSELLING BOOKS

WOMEN OF STYLE

FASHION ICONS

FASHION & STYLE

WOMEN WHO WEAR CHANEL

BEAUTY SECRETS

STYLE IN PARIS

STYLE SECRETS

THE GAME CHANGERS

LUXURY IN PARIS

BEAUTY & WELLNESS

CITATIONS D'AMOUR

DATING TIPS FOR MEN

THE JUGGLE

GOOD TO GLOW

SUCCESS SECRETS

Photography: Sheena Golani

Copyright © Steph Adams 2025

The right of Steph Adams to be identified as author of this work has been asserted in accordance with sections 77 and 78 of the Copyright, Designs and Patents Act 1988.

All rights reserved. No part of this publication may be reproduced, stored in a retrieval system, or transmitted in any form or by any means, electronic, mechanical, photocopying, recording, or otherwise, without the prior permission of the publishers.

Any person who commits any unauthorised act in relation to this publication may be liable to criminal prosecution and civil claims for damages.

A CIP catalogue record for this title is available from the British Library.

ISBN 9781035849109 (Paperback)
ISBN 9781035849116 (ePub e-book)

www.austinmacauley.com

A version of this book, co-written by Steph Adams and Samantha Brett, was published as *The Game Changers* in 2020
This revised version published 2025

Austin Macauley Publishers Ltd
1 Canada Square
Canary Wharf
London
E14 5AA